W9-CJR-234

Capturing the Whirlwind

Your Field Guide for a Successful SAP Implementation

Also available in The Whirlwind Series:

In the Path of the Whirlwind, An Apprentice Guide to the World of SAP

Capturing the Whirlwind
Your Field Guide to a Successful SAP Implementation

This book was written by Michael Doane of The Consulting Alliance, with the assistance of The Consulting Alliance partners, consultants, and project managers.

The book is dedicated to the two Managing Partners of The Consulting Alliance. To Wolfgang Beitz, who is one of the founders of The OR PARTNER Group and who had the great vision to expand the company from Europe to North America; and to Chris Carlsen, who believed from the beginning that these books had to be written, and had the grace and vision and determination to see that it would be done. It is done, and we bow our heads to the task.

"SAP" is a registered trademark of SAP Aktien-gesellschaft, Systems, Applications and Products in Data Processing, Neurottstrasse 16 69190 Walldorf, Germany. The publisher gratefully acknowledges SAP's kind permission to use its trademark in this publication. SAP AG is not the publisher of the book and is not responsible for it under any aspect of press law.

Copyright @ 1997 The Consulting Alliance, L.L.C. and OR Partner North America, L.L.C. All rights reserved

SAP is a registered trademark of SAP AG and SAP America, Inc.

All rights reserved. No part of this book may be reproduced or transmitted in any form or by any means, electronic or mechanical, including photocopying, recording, or any information storage and retrieval system, without permission in writing from the publisher.

ISBN 1-57579-030-0

Published by The Consulting Alliance, L.L.C., 101 South Main Avenue, Sioux Falls, South Dakota 57104-6423.

Printed in United States of America

PINE HILL PRESS, INC.
Freeman, S. Dak. 57029

Table of Contents

To do is to be, Aristotle

To be is to do, Sartre

Do be do be do be do, Sinatra

PREFACE

The phenomenon of SAP in North America has been the subject of countless articles in the press and SAP itself provides close to a million pages of documentation about its product. However, until our first book *In the Path of the Whirlwind, An Apprentice Guide to the World of SAP* was published, there did not exist a simple and objective source of information that would answer the basic, burning questions. What's different about SAP? Will it last? Why is it so damned expensive to implement? And on, and on.

A source book that would answer these questions was needed, so I was asked by Chris Carlsen and Wolfgang Beitz, the Managing Partners of The Consulting Alliance, to write it.

Initially, we offered the book to those who attended our executive seminars. Our intent was to keep the book brief and concise enough so that it could be read during a flight from Chicago to New York. There was no price listed because we had not considered the book as a 'sale' item, merely a solid giveaway to our clients, something more useful and cogent than a coffee mug or a key chain. To our great pleasure, we began receiving queries from people who wanted to buy additional copies. These queries multiplied as more and more copies were ordered by firms and individuals already implementing SAP or facing future SAP implementations.

We were surprised, however, to find that the book has been highly sought after by people who have already been in the SAP world for some time. We even witnessed the theft of this book by someone with three years of SAP experience. This led to some serious head scratching. Why would an experienced SAP person steal that book? We suspect that the key word in the title is "apprentice." No matter how much we know about SAP, no matter how much experience we may have, SAP is a vast and ever-expanding subject and we all feel at all times like we are still at the apprentice stage.

This second book is intended to help you past the apprentice stage and into a more comfortable zone as concerns SAP implementation projects. If you are new to SAP, we suggest that you read our other book before this one if you wish to gain full benefit of these contents. If you think you have mastered SAP... no, we doubt that anyone would think such a thing. At any rate, we intend to shed light on what has become an increasingly shady series of subjects. Scope management, consulting requirements, gap analyses, methods and tools, and countless other subjects which were seemingly mastered for classical systems implementations have not been mastered at all for SAP implementations. On the contrary, there has been considerable confusion as to how to implement this extravaganza of business functionality and workflow. The result has been high stress, wasted time, wasted money, massive disappointment, and misguided finger-pointing at SAP itself, as if the supplier can be held responsible for every blatant misuse of its product.

This book is not a methodology for an SAP implementation, nor is it a step-by-step guide because we do not believe there are any single recipe-style ways to implement SAP. We are no longer in the realm of software implementation, or the implementation of single applications. SAP is an enterprise-wide undertaking, and if the project is seriously envisioned, it will encompass every facet of your organization.

Therefore, we take the major elements of most SAP implementations and offer, in this field guide, a compass to guide your direction, a tent to keep you dry, some geezer advice for survival techniques, and more than occasional tongue-in-cheek observations about the working times in which we live.

SAP is a whirlwind, and a profitable one at that if properly addressed. So keep your eyes on the path and your matches dry.

We hope to find you at the other end of its rainbow.

Introduction

Workflow is the River; SAP is the Riverboat

Who's Afraid of SAP? Who Are You and Why Are You Reading This Book?

This book is one part cautionary tale and one part guide. And in the realm of cautionary tales, we will recount dangers and perils, we will point out the myriad species of banana peels just waiting to meet the sole of your shoes, monsters and other consultants lurking in the shadows, and the loose joints on creaky bridges from here to there.

This is not meant to discourage you, only to help you and to underscore the vast differences between an SAP implementation and all that you experienced up to now.

SAP R/3 will have been licensed about 6,000 times as this book reaches the printer. More than half of these licenses have resulted in successful implementations and the other half are in the midst of implementation to some degree or another. This book is not intended to trumpet the SAP success on a worldwide scale. If you want examples, just log into the Internet, dial SAP.COM on the Internet and check out their catalog of success stories.

As we reach into the next millenium, IS technologies are melding sweetly with telecommunications and, just as important, with new business vistas that are a radical departure from the norms that have been in place since the end of World War II.

SAP has a wide embrace, an ambitious scope that is without equal in the world market of business applications software. With SAP, and only with SAP, can a company envision having an integrated suite of applications that will run on a variety of hardware platforms in a client/server environment that allows for Internet communications, Electronic Data Interface, and ALE, all on a global (multi-currency, multi-lingual) scale.

SAP is one very tempting apple, and a multitude of companies have swept in to take a bite from it. The misfortune is that it takes far more to swallow this apple than these companies are prepared for. In 1993 and 1994, the press was all aglow about SAP, its growth, its promise, and its success. In 1995 and 1996, the press turned sour, spurred by implementation frustrations at Fortune 500 firms and by the natterings of SAP's competitors. The recurring theme of the negative press has been the duration and cost of SAP implementations. This negativism is relative to the duration and cost of other implementations. And therein lies the fallacious rub. 'Other' implementations are single application or limited linked-application implementations. Only SAP implementations are enterprise-wide, embracing the A to Z of a company. Thus sinks the comparison between an SAP implementation and 'other' implementations. Thus sink the premises of the majority of alarmist articles about the failures of SAP.

We clarify throughout this book what distinctions have to be made, preferably at the beginning of your project, between an SAP undertaking and a lesser one.

Since the early 1970s, when the first online (or real time) applications came into being, IS professionals have had to struggle with dichotomies of batch or online systems, the links (or interfaces) between applications, and the perpetual need to maintain systems as business and companies evolve. In this quarter century, business staff has seldom been content with IS support, which has been seen to lag behind true business needs. In recent years, the costs of disk, memory, telecommunications and connectivity have all fallen to fractions of what they were, but the continuing lag has been in the world of software, most specifically applications software. There are two elements of SAP that fill long-standing gaps in business evolution:

1. SAP offers a complete suite of integrated business applications

2. SAP is built and maintained by business people, not IS people.

Business applications are no longer limited to one to one to one. A full and profitable integration of finance, sales, distribution, materials management, production planning, plant maintenance and the rest are now possible.

The flow of data and the rules of processing are no longer decided or maintained by data mechanics. Business people are no longer in the back seat of that taxi; they are at the wheel.

This is a cultural revolution, not merely a business revolution. To take advantage of what SAP offers, you are invited to make the same revolution within your company. This book is not a blueprint for that revolution, it is merely a manifesto that can aid in that revolution.

Let the Stars Be Your Guide

Establishing Visible, Measurable Criteria for Success

What Am I Doing Here?

During the 1992 elections, great scorn was heaped upon Ross Perot's vice-presidential running mate, Admiral Stockdale, because he stepped forward during an idiotic debate and, with outstretched hands, asked America, "What am I doing here?" The general reading of this admiral moment was that the poor man was clueless, but we beg to differ. Given his pedigree as a professor of philosophy, not to mention the years he spent as a POW in the Hanoi Hilton, he was not clueless; he was clear-minded, and at that moment came to the realization that the debate had no real direction or value. He must have understood that he was crossing swords with a mental midget and a well-meaning lunk for the entertainment of the television audience, when he had meant to take part in a discourse of statesmen for the education of the voting public.

His question should not have been read as evidence that he was clueless. It should have been read as wisdom, a brand of wisdom which is in too short supply.

"What am I doing here?" is one of those 'take stock' questions that should be posed on a regular basis. And in the world of SAP implementations, a requisite response should be made evident at all times.

 SAP should be implemented for a reason, a clear, visible, measurable reason that can be communicated throughout an enterprise. As a company is going through the agonies of business process reengineering, some probable downsizing, and corporate bullfighting at the lofty levels (all at an incredible expense) there must be some prize at the end of the yellow brick road, an Emerald City of profit, perhaps, or the salvage of a sinking ship. A vision that is not shared will not be realized. A vision that is cloudy will give cloudy results.

Traditionally, systems projects are undertaken for business reasons: manual operations and flows require automation because of rising volume; legacy systems are outdated; management information is needed so the company can be properly steered. Just as traditionally, business has drifted, hat in hand, to systems groups to a) demand, b) negotiate, or c) beg for the needed IS support and, traditionally, IS has come through with one result or another. It is stunning, and too often disconcerting, to find that by the time 'the system' is in place, the compelling reason for that system has shifted or been lost entirely.

For an SAP implementation to truly succeed, there must be one clear, shining, intelligible, communicable, and measurable reason. Single, simple reasons for implementing SAP may not seem evident. Reasons may be as multiple as the colors of Dennis Rodman's hair, but they should not be as variable with time. If everyone in the enterprise has a clear idea of the reason behind an SAP implementation:

1. resistance to the project will be undercut;

2. business processes will adhere to one vision rather than several;

3. modifications to SAP (ABAP-style) will be less likely;

4. employees will want the implementation to succeed.

In seminars that we offer, we routinely ask attendees why their companies are going with SAP. The answers we receive are seldom enlightening. Because we were told to by a parent company. Because we have a Year 2000 (Y2K) problem and our legacy systems had to be replaced anyway. Because our parent company told us we have to. One answer given quite often: we do not know.

A second question that we always pose: does your company have a strategy? The answer is invariably 'Yes.' Somehow, we have our doubts.

The Fertilizer (or Horse Manure) of Strategic Planning

When SAP is chosen to enable a company to fulfill the strategic plan, there had better really be one to follow.

Some of the oft-quoted reasons for acquiring and implementing a new system:

*   To join the 20th century (or the newer version, to bridge to the 21st century).

- To synergize operations. (Synergy = a blending of energy and resource so that 1+1>2).

- To reduce stock.

- To improve profitability.

- To improve client service (delivery times, product quality, price).

- To streamline operations (read=downsizing).

- To reduce IS overheads.

- To integrate disparate business units (companies, divisions, etc.).

Most companies that claim to have a strategy tend to have a list comparable to the above. This is not a strategy, it is a list of good intentions. Take any item on the list and add the "how" and the "why" and assume that the brackets of an implementation period are the "when" and you will lean into strategic territory.

The fact is, it's usually about money. It could be about so much more, but make no mistake, the subject is cash and its flow. This is a concept that everyone in the company can relate to. However, too few strategies can quantify targeted savings or cash-producing initiatives. I once observed the following conversation, reproduced here almost verbatim:

Consultant:	I see that you've listed reduction of stock as item number one in your strategy for next year.
Client Exec:	That's right. We intend to reduce stocks by fifteen percent.
Consultant:	What is your current stock value?
Client Exec:	I don't know.

Consultant:	How do you plan to reduce stocks?
Client Exec:	I don't know.
Consultant:	Who will be assigned to the task?
Client Exec:	I don't know.
Consultant:	Why do you want to decrease stock levels?
Client Exec:	It seems a good practice.

The client exec wasn't wrong. Reduced stocks are "a good practice." The remainder of his 'strategy' was of the same ilk, a list of resolutions for a better-run business.

This misapplication of 'strategy' occurs all too often across the business board, and true strategic thinking is in short supply. When such fuzzy thinking is applied to any systems implementation, the results can be equally fuzzy. This will not be disastrous if we are only talking about a new stock system. It WILL be disastrous when applied to an enterprise-wide solution.

The Fog of War

We had a client whose executives bravely chose SAP as the engine to:

1. provide synergistic common systems to several companies recently united under one banner and

2. allow for a springboard into a new business dimension, not only in gross revenues but also in terms of diversification.

Other systems solutions were clearly cheaper, but all entailed significant interfacing. Client management saw clearly that once the interface apple had been bitten, interface sin would surely follow and legacy systems from all of the companies would become a major issue. Our system is better than yours, no it isn't, yes it is, let's have a meeting, no, let's have a conference.

SAP was chosen and an implementing partner from the Big 6 was agreed upon. A two-year plan was drafted, allowing for implementation in three phrases. A budget was set. In the first year:

1. an internal project manager with no SAP experience was brought in

2. the internal consultants received poor SAP training

3. the outside consultants were found lacking

4. the plan slipped by six months

5. the budget doubled

6. our firm was called in to verify the new budget and plan.

We found that the budget had not doubled. It should always have been twice what was originally established. The six-month slip was more than largely due to a silly AS-IS phase (see elsewhere in this book for more enlightenment on AS-IS phaseology), and that the new plan was for *an additional three years of implementation* (italics duly deserved).

This is what happens in the fog of war. The company had chosen SAP for a multitude of excellent reasons that were magnificently elaborated in a conference room, yet once they encountered the ruts in the road to SAP, they extended its implementation into the next millenium. (OK, a doubling of the budget is not a simple rut and the next millenium is right around the corner, but you get the point.) ROI, as in 'return on investment,' not the French word for 'king,' was suddenly lost in the shuffle of:

- understanding how to best use consultants
- incomplete SAP training
     = distrust of consultants
     = go it alone
ergo a much longer implementation period
ergo no viable return on investment until the year 2000

and relative reliance on those multiple legacy systems (and that dreaded interfacing) until the same year...

...at great cost.

Our advice was to get back onto the ROI track. This company was unlike most in that its executives were capable of clearly delineating to us what SAP would do for their company. Sadly, they had not communicated the same to the balance of the company and, worse, had lost sight of their aims in the midst of the struggle.

The point of this mini case study is that even companies which begin an SAP implementation for all the right, clear, and measurable reasons may, in the fog of war, lose sight of the measurable, attainable benefits, and drift into longer, less-cost-per-year, implementations.

What did they do? Half of what we told them to do: a) abandon the go-it-alone approach and find decent SAP consultants to provide impetus, most especially regarding integration points; b)seek out proper training, rare as it is. They did not c) accelerate the implementation to grasp the benefits and thus reap those benefits, or d) communicate the project vision to the rest of the company.

Advil time.

Visible, Measurable Criteria for SAP Success

I once was project manager for a French tire manufacturer (yes, the same one that has the slogan *nunc bibendum est/now is the time to drink* and that smiling, bug-eyed fat thing as a marketing image). If ever there was a project with visible, measurable criteria for success, this was it.

Tires were supplied to Japanese car manufacturers for OEM and each of these manufacturers were of course following JIT principles. The client's difficulties were based on a single, simple point:

> *All tires, whether produced in Europe or America, were on an 11-week supply chain, including delivery by ship and supplier data (sales forecasting, supply chain monitoring, and ordering) was in disarray.*

In the tire business, original equipment tires lead to the subsequent sale of 2.2 replacement tires, so if the client missed delivery of one tire, they not only lost face with the auto makers, they also lost business for altogether 3.2 tires to a rival supplier. This latter point was the least important. The patience of the auto makers had been stretched very thin and business was suffering as a whole.

To stem the tide, the company was handing 12% of its annual revenue to Air France to airlift needed stock. As the story goes, one 747 once carried twelve tires from Paris to Tokyo.

The project mission: to radically reduce the Air France bill while still providing customer service in a JIT environment. This is a *prime* example of visible and measurable criteria for success.  Although this was not an easy project by any stretch of the imagination, our project team did have the benefit of knowing clearly what was at the end of the rainbow. Design decisions all adhered to a vision of providing the client company the means to reduce the Air France bill and fulfill customer turnaround requirements. There were no lengthy meetings on the subject of priorities or direction or strategy. Managing the scope of the project was simplified through the same means. If a proposed add-on to the project did not advance the same vision, it was rejected.

Not all projects offer such simple targets. All the same, finding yours, at the onset of your implementation, will have lasting repercussions, and benefits.

What to look for:

- a reduction of effort, whether with fewer people or through a re-alignment of processes into a workflow

- an increase in production

- better visibility of results = information.

This last point is often difficult to quantify compared to the other two. All the same, if you are going to succeed in your implementation, provide your team and the company a tangible goal, not just some fuzzy buzz phrase.

The reason behind a project should also be grounded in the truth. When the Vietnam War was being fought because of the Domino Theory (i.e. if Saigon fell, the commies would then attack Hawaii and then San Diego and, gosh, Omaha). This rationale did not withstand serious scrutiny, and there was some serious resistance to that project and none of its project managers came out of it with a bonus and a new watch.

By the same token, the success criteria had better be attractive. If, prior to D-Day, General Eisenhower had told his men they were storming the beaches of Normandy so that a film festival could be established at Deauville, it's doubtful that the attack would have succeeded.

Look for what is intrinsic and obvious and quantifiable and you will win your D-Day.

A final reminder:

It is not SAP that is going to provide the benefit. Gains will be *enabled* by SAP as by no other applications suite on the planet, but the gains have to be engineered by you and your company. If you expect that by simply implementing SAP you will reap the harvest, you are mistaken.

A Postscript:

SAP, the Balm to Salve Old IS Budget War Wounds

Why do so many companies measure IS costs as a percentage of gross revenues? What is the meaning of this? We see stats all the time about companies that did x and, as part of the benefit, saw IS costs tumble from 2.5 % of gross revenues to 2.2% or some such thing. There is no magic thread that can be spun to determine if reduction of IS costs is profit-effective. IS, as a cost, can reduce other costs. Name another service within a company that can make the same claim. Marketing brings revenue. Sales bring revenue. IS reduces costs, both in operational and human terms. Imagine, for a moment, how many more armies of people it would take for your company to do what it does if there were no IS, no computers, none of those techies in the house whatsoever. Add it up. Any of you reading this who are in the IS world and have butted heads with people anxious to chop your budget because you are an overhead will empathize. IS is not an overhead, you are telling them, it is an opportunity. They just can't see it. So, back to the project-justification spreadsheets and the PowerPoint presentation to back it all up.

Since most CEOs still tend to look at SAP as an IS cost, how can they measure a reduction of IS costs as part of the benefits package? Simple. SAP rationally reduces IS costs by shifting the emphasis to business and away from support overheads.

Rent is an overhead. Stationery, travel costs, plumbing. SAP is a cost cutter while being a workflow enabler. Spend to win.

Instant SAP Gratification

A Scenario for Rapid Acquisition, Training, and Implementation of SAP

Grab the Software *Before* Designing the Processes

If you have already decided to go ahead with SAP, you may wish to skip this section and go on to the implementation guidelines. If you are still looking for the right software solution and SAP is only one of your options, read on.

Traditionally, companies in need of new software systems have followed a left-to-right path: 1) design the new business processes then 2) find the package that fits them most closely. In the same tradition, it is presumed that no package will fit more than 80% of a company's needs, and so the remaining elusive,  unique-to-you, 20% has to be designed and developed separately.

Too often, companies have failed to forge ahead with new software acquisition because of an obsession over that 20%. Instead of looking at the broader picture of how a new and dynamic 80% solution will improve company performance, they have waited, or searched for a package that just might do it all.

Besides the dithering, it is the design process (or the drafting of detailed specifications) that has traditionally slowed system acquisition and implementation. You know the scenario: you huddle with your systems people, putting pencil to paper, defining how your systems should work for you, then you go out and visit the vendors to see if there isn't a package that will fit, find that there aren't any, reconsider your specification, settle on a vendor, and then simultaneously acquire the new software and develop the missing 20% and *then* write the interfaces to any surviving legacy systems *as well as* the 20% you've developed to fulfill the specification.

The theory is that you will now have 100% satisfactory systems, meeting the needs as specified way back when. The fact of the matter is that you will have perhaps a 90% fit because a) business requirements are constantly changing and b) you have a data base that is interfaced, not integrated.

In sum, much of the specification writing/design has been redundant to the far more elaborate designs of the vendors and is largely wasted time.

Until recently, there was not much way around that scenario. But with the availability of integrated package suites and client/server technology, data access and presentation are no longer an issue. And with SAP, the applications themselves are both flexible and comprehensive.

The point is, you should now reconsider the traditional approach to package acquisition. Do not look for a package to support your design, look for a package suite that will be a platform upon which you will reengineer your company. And in the case of this exercise, that package suite will be SAP.

What are the Implementation Steps?

If you stick around an SAP environment long enough, you will undoubtedly hear certain phrases repeated over and over again. "Integration is the key to SAP." "Business reengineering is the key to SAP." "SAP is simpler than it appears to be; only the configuration is complex." Another of these phrases, repeated like a mantra throughout an SAP implementation, is:

> AN SAP R/3 IMPLEMENTATION IS NOT A COMPUTER PROJECT BUT A BUSINESS PROJECT

Cut this out and tape it your laptop screen. This phrase is repeated because the steps so commonly known for standard software projects do not apply for an SAP implementation. Methodologies for design and development of new systems or the implementation of best-of-breed software will include phases and tasks that are of no import to an SAP project. This phrase is true primarily because the emphasis of an SAP implementation is the **business** process re-design, not the design of the system that will support those processes.

To take it a step further:

> AN SAP R/3 IMPLEMENTATION IS NOT A DIVISIONAL COMPUTER PROJECT BUT AN ENTERPRISE-WIDE BUSINESS PROJECT

Previous experience in IS projects can be more harmful than helpful if project members insist upon doing things as they have in the past. The following is a thumbnail sketch of the differences you will encounter.

Classical Software Project	SAP Project
Cater to individual divisions or departments	Address the company as a whole
Address incremental evolution	Force radical evolution
Software development is the primary activity (IS dominated)	Business reengineering is the primary activity (business dominated)
Project method is step by step and linear	Project method is iterative and interactive
IS and Users negotiate design	Users define usage

While perusing consulting firms' brochures, you will undoubtedly come across a variety of charts describing implementation steps, some of them the wallpaper box and quiver of arrows variety which list detail tasks over a three-year period. Some methods place more emphasis on SAP functionality than process redesign (or vice versa) while others focus on streamlining company processes. In the world of SAP consulting, there are a plethora of 'methods' that incorporate adjectives suggesting implementation *speed*: rapid, swift, quick, instant. As if the implementation of a revolutionary, wall-busting complete applications suite can be compared to the grilling and bagging of cheeseburgers. The title of this chapter is meant to be tongue-in-cheek. There is no instant R/3 gratification. It takes time to implement, whatever method is employed. Beyond the implementation tasks, it takes time for your staff to orient themselves to the new business world around them. This orientation cannot happen in a matter of weeks, so look askance upon implementation methods that may rush the job rather than complete the job.

The bottom line is: There is no single acceptable approach that must be adopted for an SAP implementation and anyone who tells you so is the kind of person who tells you there's only one car worth owning, only one beer worth drinking, and only one woman worth loving.

All the same, nearly all SAP implementations include the following elements or actions.

	ACTION	DECISION
	The Critical Event	SAP goes in; hell or high water
1	Envision the future	What will change?
2	Create Implementation Plan	Phased or Big Bang?
3	Form Your Team	Who will do what?
4	Install SAP	What pre-configuration?
5	Define SAP Hierarchies	Information architecture?
6	Redesign Processes	How will you work?
7	Configure SAP	How will it work for you?
8	Train Users	Who are the users?
9	System Migration	How to switch over?
10	Use the Systems	Monitor Benefits Realization

For the most part, these steps occur in a linear fashion, with some overlapping and some serious looping for steps 6 and 7. The one point that will actually be addressed through all phases of the project is training.

The Critical Event

The CEO, or anyone else with real power (clout, the hammer), has the vision that SAP will be a cost cutting, streamlining, upgrading, inspiring, and evolutionary software platform to thrust your company into the next millennium. The word gets out. Confetti fills the air.

Envision the Future

This the first and most outlandish step in an SAP project. Dreaming isn't normally allowed in a business environment, but "that's how we do things 'round here" is an answer that will no longer suffice.

Now you are invited to imagine a company that works in the best possible fashion. This is the keynote phase to the reengineering process and this step should be approached as if you were starting the company over again.

This is not a tinkering phase or a time to simply fine-tune. You should be looking at your company from a fresh point of view, with a focus on:

- Why does your company do what it does?

- What are your strategic goals? Why have you considered implementing SAP?

- What changes will likely produce the most dramatic benefits?

- Where are the points of resistance to change and how can that resistance be eliminated?

Questions such as these should be asked at each level of the organization, in a descending fashion down the entire pyramid: company, sector, division, department, function. The current company structure should also be questioned, so that process redesign can occur on a diagonal, wall-busting plane. The SAP software that will support your new business processes is a diagonal application, meaning that it supports entire business processes that cross departmental boundaries and company hierarchies.

Let us return to that phrase 'diagonal, wall-busting plane.' It sounds smooth, and will look smooth on a project plan, but the fact is that a diagonal, wall-busting plane is just what most people will resist because it not only affects the way they will be working, it may also affect them right out of their jobs or into new positions altogether. SAP implementations do not *require* this kind of re-structuring in all cases, but it can be an obvious result of serious business process reengineering intended to give both the company and SAP a chance to work some magic.

In a serious effort, the decision-making will be redistributed, and it is in this arena that you will find the highest level of resistance. Some staff will resent a loss of power and others will shy away from new responsibilities. The cultural changes will be surprising and, at least initially, bewildering.

It is not necessary to find the perfect plan for a perfect set of business processes. At this stage in the project, you should be working in headlines, with the smaller print of actual process redesign to occur later. If you start spinning your wheels at this juncture, the project will bog down.

Create an Implementation Plan

In establishing the scope of the project, you will be laying the groundwork toward answers to innumerable implementation questions that must be addressed in the plan. Scope factors include:

- How many sites, company entities and users are envisioned?

- What legacy systems will be retained? Temporarily or permanently? What interfaces will be required?

23

- How vital is the elusive 20%? Must it be addressed in the first level of implementation? (The answer to this question is usually a firm 'No,' but there will be more meetings over these issues than most project managers can bear.)

- What are the maximum benefits that can be obtained by using SAP? Whatever is required to realize these benefits should be at the center of the project scope.

The drafted implementation plan will address a major decision, the consequences of which cannot be overstated: how will you implement? In staged phases (often referred to as a rollout) or all at once, i.e. Big Bang? If only the answers were as simple as the phrases.

ROLLOUT	BIG BANG
Some functions can be implemented quickly	Implement only when all business units are ready
Tighter focus during initial system use	System use is widespread
Some integration is delayed	Integration is immediate
Temporary interfaces need to be written	No interfaces are needed
Medium risk	Medium to high risk

In a rollout implementation, individual functions or processes go live one or two at a time until all functions are fully implemented. Some rollouts are geographic based (site by site), others are domain based (finance first, then sales & distribution, then materials management, etc.), and others are necessity based, such as when some business units are ready to implement ahead of others. In a Big Bang implementation, all functions and processes go live at the same time. Whichever of these scenarios you choose, the resulting implementation plan must have milestones (or deadlines, if we have to use the word) which can be achieved and a project flow which can be measured on a daily basis.

For the purpose of brevity, we will not detail each of these task groups, which are, at any rate, self-evident. The time-line and project duration will vary depending upon the size of the company, number of users, implementation type, and number and type of applications being installed.

Form Your Team

Having developed the vision, you will now be in a position to form a team that can pursue that vision. For classical systems projects, this team would consist of a project manager, some systems analysts, user representatives, and an assortment of analyst and programming techies. IS top-heavy, in short. For an SAP project, the balance should be quite different, teaming business people from your company with outside consultants who should be more business-oriented than IS-laden. In classical systems, teams were like baseball teams, with business at bat first, followed by analysts, then programmers, then analysts for the testing, then business again for acceptance testing.

For an SAP implementation, the team is more like a combination of football, in which everyone has to work together. The relationship between outside consultants and internal implementers is somewhat like doubles tennis in which each member will bring forth strengths and be compensated by a teammate for weaknesses.

Consider the following staff chart:

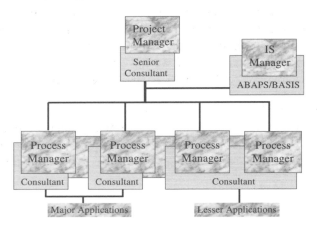

Under this scheme, your staff is composed of process managers, each entrusted with responsibility for a specific application (or suite of applications). The process managers will master the functional aspects and have an understanding of the integration points for the module. In smaller companies, it may be possible to have one person managing a suite of applications, such as SD through MM.

At the beginning of the project, each process manager would have a "shadow" consultant, either part-time or full time depending upon the scope. These consultants should bring their SAP experience and insight and the process managers should instigate the transfer of knowledge at the outset.

Note that these process managers should not be IS staff, but business staff from the departments relative to the applications. In addition to communication skills, clarity of thought, expertise in consensus building, a taste for change, boundless enthusiasm, a Mercedes laptop with all the gizmos, a dazzling wardrobe, fast car, and extreme patience, the process managers must also have *power*. They must be in a position to implement new business processes and practices, and to make decisions that will enable the company to use SAP as the enabler of those processes. If they are merely viewed as "coordinators," with little back-up from senior management, the exercise may resemble The University of (Insert Your Company Name), in which your company has been the subject of many term papers leading to no appreciable improvement.

Another point that must be clear as regards these people: they must have the time to devote to the project. Process managers should be assigned full-time and associated staff will inevitably have to be assigned at least half of their time or the project will definitely drift.

IS functions must be coordinated by an IS leader dedicated to the SAP project on a full-time basis. This individual should not have to toggle time between the SAP project and current systems. IS activities in the project may include some custom programming in ABAP/4 to fill functional gaps and, with shadow consulting available, your IS staff should be fully trained to BASIS and ABAP/4 programming.

At some point during the project, you should be able to lower the ratio of consulting time to in-house time. Remember that the aim is to use the consultants to provide knowledge and experience at the onset, and to transfer that knowledge and experience to your company.

At this point, a basic implementation plan should be established for the remaining phases of the project. After the next phase (installing SAP), the implementation plan can be fleshed out to task level. It is not advisable to attempt the creation of a highly detailed master plan prior to acquiring and installing SAP unless your team is also familiar with the pre-configured software you will be installing.

This is also a time when training should begin. This plan is not entirely linear, so you may want to jump ahead, briefly, to the section on training for some guidelines.

Install SAP ASAP

This certainly sounds easier than it seems because the installation process with SAP can take its own eternity. SAP provides only a fair amount of installation support, relying instead on its third party partners (i.e. platform and/or consulting firms) to provide the  help needed. That is why your team should already be in place.

To shorten and rationalize the inevitable configuring process, you should be looking toward installing a pre-configured "vanilla" system. By "vanilla," we mean a system configured generically enough so that the most common and frequent standard transactions are in place. By pre-configured, we mean that the basic configuration to be installed will fit the industry field in which you are working. In order to locate a pre-configured system, contact either SAP or the ICOE for your sector (more on this later). Failing that, find a company or two as similar to your own that are already using SAP and see if you can arrange something.

Do not install a basic, factory-packaged SAP if at all possible. Much of the subsequent configuration work would be unnecessarily complex and time-consuming. Invest your time searching for a configuration that someone else has puzzled over and carry on from there. The time spent investigating previously-accomplished configurations will pay off with a huge time savings in later implementation stages.

Define SAP Hierarchies

This can be the most painful part of an entire SAP process, because it strikes at the heart of how your company works. Companies with a high degree of vertical organization, in which various divisions have worked with great autonomy, find that SAP is "forcing" them to cross toward a more horizontal approach. Divisions that have been run as mini empires are difficult to bring into the SAP integrated scheme.

At issue is the hierarchy by which reporting, costing, and controls will be established. Some companies skirt this issue by running multiple SAPs for different business entities. These companies have invested megabucks for integrated systems and then decided to skip the integration, so let's assume that this isn't a recommended path. More enlightened companies struggle further with the hierarchy to take advantage of the horizontal approach to the reporting and data sharing concepts. At base, SAP seeks to create financial control across the spectrum, in which each business unit (division, group, office) can be viewed as a cost or profit center. What becomes a sticking point is that there is only *one* data base, no matter how many kingdoms have been established or how many presentation servers are installed.

Note: this one data base factor is supposed to be eliminated with version 3.1 in which SAP will be split into three components of logistics, finance, and human resources. Components will be able to function as discrete application suites or be linked up to one another with the traditional single database.

The project cannot continue successfully until the hierarchy is firmly established and agreed upon. Thus, management holds the key. If the higher ups do not participate in the establishment of this hierarchy, resistance will perpetuate. Many an SAP implementation has foundered on just these rocks.

Some companies prefer creating an operational model or prototype once the project scope has been firmly established and new business processes have been mapped. The existence of a working model can pay huge dividends, including:

- A consequential, or parallel, gap analysis will occur and you will identify what functions or features SAP will not satisfy.

- "Proving" the desirability of implementing by offering a scale model of a working system (with defined processes) to people who are resisting the project.

- A first detailed view of your future workload will result and the project plan can be refined.

Sandboxing is a term that is sometimes used, and the image applies. What you are doing is building a sand castle. If it is not to your liking, you have only to knock it down and start again. The prototype can be changed throughout an iterative reengineering phase until an "ideal" model is agreed upon.

Before going on to business process reengineering, we feel compelled to add a firm note in regard to your gap analysis. A huge waste of time and money result when consultants or clients   jump to hasty conclusions about what R/3 will or will not do for them. The easy reflex is to plan for add-on programming or, worse, the acquisition of other software that can be patched in to fulfill a function that R/3 ostensibly cannot satisfy.

The error is that at this point in the project, your staff certainly doesn't know enough about R/3 to make this call and your consultants may very well be in the same leaky boat. Therefore, let that gap analysis just simmer for a while. If you rush to address each identified gap, especially with 'inserted' new software, you will be losing much of what you purchased in the first place, namely the integration. Later in the project, when your knowledge of R/3 has deepened and widened, you will find that a number of those perceived gap issues will simply slide off the page. There *will* be functions and features that R/3 won't deliver, but you also have to ask yourself if the value of those functions outweighs the cost in time, money, and loss of R/3 integrity. Much more on this subject is to come.

Reengineer Business Processes

There is no way to relate, in a few words, all that you need to know about the reengineering of business processes. This is a subject that can require volumes to cover properly. We definitely recommend that anyone contemplating the acquisition and implementation of SAP should become versed in the principles and practice of process reengineering. Toward that end, we offer some of the basics.

1. Process reengineering is not the modifying or streamlining of existing business processes. Rather, it is the re-creation of business processes, at a fundamental level, with the purpose of radically improving the company in terms of its customer service or its economic posture, or both.

2. A business process is not an isolate element such as a task, an input, or an output. It is a suite of activities that culminate in output or a result that brings added value to the customer. An example is a process that begins with the receipt of an order from a customer,

continues to the customer's receipt of goods, and ends with payment of those goods.

3. Be certain that the process managers will be given full responsibility for individual processes. It is they who have to have to sell new ideas to resistors and see the reengineering to its finish. These individuals will logically have sufficient clout and credibility within the organization; if not, even the most brilliantly conceived new processes may not be successfully implemented.

You begin with the assumption, generally true, that SAP offers the integrated functionality and system performance necessary to support the new organization that you've envisioned. Thus, at this point, you go about the detail of describing the great new business world that your company will become.

The descriptions can take many forms, but the most useful for an SAP implementation are visual depictions, such as process charts and data flow charts. SAP R/3 includes a working tool called the Analyzer, and although the user world is split on the advisability of using it, one can only wonder why the hesitation, if not for the fact that this tool is somewhat misunderstood. In the next section, the R/3 Reference Model is discussed. At this point in the project, the Analyzer could be used to chart existing business processes and, consequently, new and desired business processes.

Taken together, the Analyzer and the Reference Model and other small components are nowadays referred to as the Business Engineering Workbench. We refuse to comment one way or another on the tools that you will choose. ARIS offers another version of this same capability, as do other suppliers like Visio. We listen to heated debates as to merits of each of these and we can only shrug. One man's hammer is another woman's baseball bat. We will leave this choice to you.

For a raring-to-go company, charting current business processes may be only a huge waste of time. In essence, you could spend weeks or months documenting a business structure you intend to demolish. Best to carry on and start modeling the future.

However, a company struggling to come up with a vision for new business processes may find it instructive to chart existing processes with the Analyzer. Redundant activities and pointless processes would be rendered visible and the charts themselves will provide a shorthand for discussion.

Whichever way you decide to go, it is now essential that your business processes be fixed, not simply changed. Avoid the buzzwords and abstractions such as *empowerment, synergy, teaming,* et al and concentrate on cause and effect. Each new business process should have an identified trigger (a customer calls with an order) and an identified consequence, or series of consequences (the order is entered into the system, a confirmation issued, and a stock request sent). In turn, a given consequence will be a trigger in another process.

What you are searching for is workflow, an acceleration of business processes through the elimination of unnecessary worker intervention or system dead ends. You are also searching for automated connections to both clients and suppliers (think Electronic Data Interchange; think Internet).

Failures will occur, and should not be punishable by death. Each radical change carries risk, and these risks should be measured against anticipated benefits.

BPR and R/3 configuration lie squarely on the critical path of an R/3 implementation, and these two activities are linked and iterative. Repeat, iterative. Repeat, iterative. Repeat...oh, sorry.

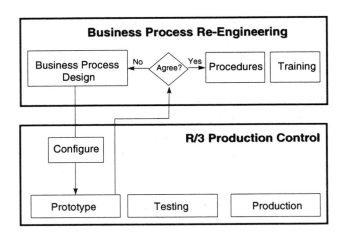

This is the point at which too many methodologies, linear in scope, bog down. An R/3 implementation is a series of bubbles that have to be burst, curlicues, not straight lines. Configuration logically follows BPR, and in many cases, configuration failures lead to new BPR or new items in the gap analysis that may have to be addressed with ABAP/4 add-ons. Some companies are tempted to accelerate the process by leaving configuration to the consultants while speeding ahead with BPR. This is not advisable. Your staff should be taking the lead in the configuring process so that once the consultants are gone, you will find yourselves firmly at the wheel.

Our friend and colleague, Jim O'Keefe, likens R/3 to an erector set, his principle being that you have all the pieces you need to build whatever you want and as long as you do not bend the pieces (i.e. modify the base code), you can re-build what you will later want with the same pieces. The configuring process is therefore comparable to choosing your pieces and settling how they will fit together. It is what happens with an R/3 implementation, this fitting together of parts. BPR only provides part of what you will need. Familiarity with SAP R/3 is the other essential.

Configure SAP

In the years since R/3 was announced, the perception (and sometimes painful reality) has been that SAP takes an eternity to implement. When interviewed, people complain about two aspects in particular: reengineering (which is their turf) and configuring (which is SAP's). The configuration is the process by which functions are tailored to your requirements: screen layouts and masking, data flows, the rules of processing, etc.

There are literally thousands of configuration options and sorting through them to fit the system to your business processes can be mind-numbing and time-consuming. This is the other edge of the SAP broadsword. There is quite simply so much functionality and flexibility built into the system that mere mortals cannot keep up.

To this point, you have the "vanilla-preconfigured" version and a new and detailed configuring map based upon your new business process designs. It is not an obligation to complete the configuration to the last detail before implementing. This is where so very many implementations hit the skids and the whirlwind of design-configure-design-configure turns SAP projects into three-way mudwrestling matches between implementers, users, and the system itself.

The product (or, to use the 80s term, 'deliverable') of BPR and configuring is the prototype. An SAP prototype is a proof of concept that is visible to anyone who has the time to look at it. With a prototype, you can 'walk through' whole processes to test them, and you can continue to build upon them until your whole corporate world learns to sing in the same key.

Our earnest advice is to seek a cut-off point at which individual and detail requirements be set aside and system migration be allowed to commence. Once SAP is in production, the configuration process can go on.

Addressing this daunting facet of its existence, SAP has come up with a variety of solutions and tools:

The R/3 Reference Models

With this tool, you can create and modify the components and flow of various business processes (referred to as "event-driven process chains" or EPCs) within the system. This considerably eases confusion, since the EPCs are depicted in simple and clear flow charts of events (i.e. the customer calls in a sales order) and functions (sales order entry) and the configuring process is not simply a series of codes and switches.

Once the Reference Model is satisfactory, you can use the R/3 Procedure Model which describes all of the tasks involved in an implementation, including the dependencies between project stages and work steps, standard settings, and recommendations. The Reference Model will serve

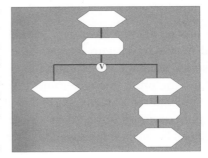

as a companion to the Procedure Model; between these two, the documentation, on-line help, training materials, data models, and process models are integrated.

In all, the Reference Model allows for system depiction at five levels. In addition to process view, are:

- Information flow, describing the relationships and attributes between senders and receivers of information.

- Data models showing data entities that are key to company activities (as depicted in the process flows). Though different data levels can be viewed, only the first level of detail is required for business definitions.

- Function viewing will show a snapshot/chart of the company's defined hierarchy. This is a static view, changed only according to the hierarchical definition.

- Organization, in which certain organizational relationships are delineated.

R/3 Pre-Set Configurations

Given the large number of R/3 installations in existence, the live configurations of R/3 are multiplying. SAP has been gathering a library of diverse configuration sets for some time and customers are invited to take any of these and apply them directly if so desired.

If you use the SAP customizing tools or take a pre-set configuration, you can drastically reduce the implementation time and get your company up and running on SAP. Despite the continual complaints about lengthy implementations, dozens of companies have implemented all or part of SAP in mere months. The reasons for success vary, but one constant has been management determination in the realm of configuring the system to meet the defined business processes and not getting stuck in office politics, power struggles, and the like. Companies that are taking an eternity to implement SAP should, in many cases, stop harping about the configuration logjam and focus instead upon the preceding business process issues.

Educate Your Staff

Education is an ongoing concern throughout the duration of an SAP implementation, and it is one of the thornier issues in an SAP project. Instrutors are varied in skills and finding adequate training (the right course for the right individual at the right time) is not a simple task.

There are three levels of education to be addressed:

1.   management education

2.   implementation team education

3.   user training.

Later in this book, we devote an entire chapter to SAP education and will therefore not offer details here. Suffice to say, education will be required at all times and at nearly all levels of your enterprise. It will not be limited to teaching users what keystrokes to use to obtain their desired ends.

For the implementation team, SAP product training can be arranged through the SAP offices throughout the country. This training can be made to focus on specific functions (Sales & Distribution, Production Planning, et al). Unfortunately, the people who provide this training are often professional trainers, not people with actual SAP flight logs.

Industry Centers of Expertise were instituted in 1995 to act as liaison between SAP and customers in various sectors. Typical of SAP, they are referred to as ICOEs but that's more initials-identity obsession. These centers provide assistance in finding configuration sets and providing working models to fit individual company needs, and are divided into:

Automotive	Consumer Packaged Goods
HealthCare	Financial Service Industry
Oil and Gas	High Tech/Electronics
Process Industries	Utilities & Communications

Operation Jumpstart commenced in May of 1994. It consists of an overview class for all team members, and then special sessions for specific fields of interest (SD, FI, what have you). SAP is offering new courses focusing on the ASAP methodology starting in the Spring of 1997. These courses are available on a regular basis in Atlanta, Chicago, Foster City, Philadelphia, and Toronto, and new sites have been added, including Boston, Dallas, Calgary, Montreal, Cleveland, Cincinnati, St. Louis, Minneapolis, and Irvine, California. More are sure to be added. Check with your SAP representative for the site closest to you. Further education will be required, and at various levels for various team members.

Project managers should master system architecture (particularly as it pertains to the hierarchy), tools (ARIS, Navigator, et al for customizing and reengineering), and the ins and outs of configuring.

Process managers should seek training at the SAP centers for the areas in which they will be responsible.

Company management should receive considerable overview and training to SAP as well, even though full-time project involvement may not be planned. Think of top management as the 'owners' of business processes. Final decisions relative to re-engineering will be theirs, so a familiarity with SAP on an organizational level will be needed.

Later on in the project, user training will occur. By user training, we mean the training of those people who will actually be touching the system on a daily basis. In order to eliminate dependence upon SAP and/or those pricey consultants, you should consider establishing a three-generational scheme for initial training: A consultant teaches your manager all about a function. The manager teaches the users. One user is assigned as ongoing internal training consultant. There are other variants, including the notion of including Super Users within the configuring team. Either approach is viable. Flip of a coin.

Throughout the life cycle of the system, on-line help and on-line documentation are available, but these features are not always as helpful as you would like, and nothing can replace one-to-one tutoring.

What is important is that your own staff master the functions as soon as possible and as completely as possible, so that you will not be dependent upon consultants for the ongoing use of the system. Again, the **transfer of knowledge** is the key here (that is why it is always in bold).

In summary, training options include:

- SAP-specific training companies (refer to the last pages of this book)

- Industry Centers of Expertise

- SAP training through SAP America (individual course offerings are throughout the year)

- Consultant training, if truly qualified consultants can be found

- Send an employee to a company already using SAP for training

- Intensive use of on-line documentation and on-line help.

System Migration

Whichever implementation route you have chosen, rollout or Big Bang, each of the business modules will now migrate from legacy systems to SAP. The order in which this migration occurs is up to company needs and strategy, but logical system segments should be migrated together if integration is an issue. For example, all applications relative to order fulfillment (SD and probably MM and maybe PP) may need to be migrated at the same time. Human Resources (HR) might best be implemented first in order to facilitate eventual workflow.

Have we already made it clear that we view interfacing as an evil that should be avoided wherever possible? If the implementation is the rollout variety, interfaces cannot be avoided, since links between SAP and legacy systems will be required. As final implementation nears, some departments of your company will be more prepared than others and the temptation to settle on interfaces (temporarily, of course) will be strong. Avoid this temptation. Interfacing to SAP is complex and time-consuming and the more of it you do, the longer you put off final implementation.

It may be better to live with a number of *manual* processes for a determined period than to undertake an elaborate interfacing subproject. Legacy systems that are not destined for the scrap heap will require interfacing. Nothing's perfect in life. Go ahead.

Know When You're Finished and Say So

If you have followed a well-constructed implementation plan, knowing the point at which it has been fulfilled will be relatively easy. SAP R/3 will be running in most of your divisions, output will be flowing, and the company will have already begun to reap the anticipated benefits. You should be prepared to invoke the 80 percent rule, having reached critical mass. Your business is running and that other twenty percent will be a daily, constant shifting target, so if the transfer of knowledge has been successful, boot out those consultants and get on with your business.

We do not mean to dictate your behavior at this or at any point in the project, but at this point, please, let everyone know that you have reached the end. Make it a celebration, not just another day at the racetrack. Obviously, there will be kinks to work out, processes to be reconsidered, software to be patched in, but this will always be the case. Having SAP up and running doesn't qualify everyone for early retirement, except the consultants if you haven't yet thanked them, toasted them, and politely shown them the door.

Internal staff that has been assigned full time to the SAP project can now ride off into the sunset and resume their former lives, though some will prefer to continue with SAP in some capacity, while others will be headhunted right out of your company and into consulting if their efforts (and newly-acquired SAP expertise) are not recognized.

Post implementation tactics will vary depending upon the level of success of the implementation. Now is the time to return to those intentions and visions of the first step and measure how closely you have come to achieving them. It is also a time for new vision, a return to the beginning of the system life cycle, but this time rippling with SAP muscle.

A New Vision of the System Life Cycle

The life cycle of an information system has traditionally been viewed as circular:

- the perception of a need
- planning
- acquisition/development
- implementation and utilization
- degradation = the growing perception of a need

Once SAP is implemented, the system may no longer follow this pattern. Add-on modules and upgrades may always be needed, as well as that elusive twenty percent. But for the core of your business (and a large core at that) you should not find it necessary to redesign or replace software. As needs arise and the performance of the system is found wanting, your company may find it advantageous to re-engineer business processes and reflect changes in the SAP configuration.

Over the River and Through the Woods: The Aerial View

Planning Your SAP Implementation

Why Is Planning for SAP So Different?

If you think of planning as the charting of a path from the promise of A to the fulfillment of Z, you assume that the mountains to be scaled and the streams to be forded have been seen before and charted by wizened fellas with steely eyes and solid flowcharting skills. And in the case of acquisition, development, and implementation of classical systems, that much is largely true. There are dozens of development methodologies that can be faithfully followed which will lead you from the rocks to the shore with a modicum of certainty. From Method 1 to Summit D to whatever is touted in the shiniest of the consulting brochures that you can lay your hands on, if you are talking about a single application, go right ahead and follow the dotted lines. You are in known territory and even the earthworms along the footpath have been inventoried.

45

But along comes SAP, and you may as well take every one of those maps/methodologies and use their binders as kindling for a warm fire. The SAP winds blow cold and those earthworms are now snakes and what once was a stream is now a rushing river so those methodologies will not help one bit. You are working on an enterprise-wide scale now, and what you need is a brand new form of cartography.

 Methodologies are mostly linear and will lead you from A to Z in a step-to-step fashion. But SAP implementations are literally filled with iterative, loopy, bottleneck points that need to be seen, at the outset, from an aerial view, not from ground level.

Behold the factors of an SAP implementation that behoove this:

1. The Effects of the Learning Curve

Few companies launch an SAP implementation with adequate knowledge of what they are about to attempt. Indeed, a number of companies fail once, step back and gain further education, and then begin anew. Of all the factors necessary for a successful implementation, SAP education is number two. Number one, as mentioned frequently, is management commitment.

2. The Inclusion of Business Staff

In the traditional, non-SAP methodologies, business staff plays the role of client, asking for what it wants and then approving or rejecting whatever IS can come up with.

In an SAP project, IS is largely on the sidelines, whereas business staff is at the wheel. It is one thing to estimate the time needed for a team of programmers to code up a new accounting system and another thing to estimate the time necessary for an army of business people, often still embroiled in *current* business, to configure a customer order processing workflow. This is vastly new territory to almost any enterprise and we have yet to see a methodology that can address it.

3.   The Duration of the Implementation

Installing a new accounting system, in even the most difficult environment, might take six months, two of which would be spent convincing the bean counters that they will get all the same reports and listings as their beloved mainframe has always provided.

Installing a new manufacturing system in certain process industries can take a year or more depending upon the ambition of the project.

Installing SAP....no, wait. We do not *install* SAP, we subscribe to SAP, we take it on the way a priest takes on his robes. And in some enterprises, this adoption can take more than a year (or much, much more). At this writing, General Motors is still mulling the decision. If the answer is GO, we imagine a ten year project in the making, give or take a Tampa Bay Buccaneers winning season.

SAP implementations take time, and for good reason. The entire life cycle of an enterprise is scrutinized, argued over, taken to task, tested, tasted, and either digested or spit out. There are countless articles in the press about how to shorten the cycle of SAP implementations, and this same chapter addresses the subject, but the fact of the matter is that you are not breaking eggs to make an omelet, you are breaking a case or three of eggs to make an omelet mountain. And there will always be a gallery of chickens to cluck at you about your method for breaking those eggs.

It is one thing to plan a three-month project that will result in a new spare parts stock system and quite another to plan an eighteen-month project that will change the course of your company for at least the coming five years.

4. The Iterative Process of BPR to Configuration to BPR to Configuration Until the Prototype Holds Water

Many business processes, no matter how complex, fit squarely into R/3 configurations. That is one of the charms of SAP, and one of its strengths. But other processes that you may need turn into Chinese puzzles of configuration and, as you configure, you are led back to the BPR drawing board more than once. You will not be able to simply lay out your processes, configure SAP to meet them, and move on. There will be a loop, a return from configuration to BPR and back again until your prototype is satisfactory. How you define 'satisfactory' and how long you take to get there will have a major impact on your master plan (and your nervous system).

5. The Stakes

Already stated: enterprise-wide, as in the whole company. Everyone is affected, and the bottom line can become hard to find.

If you succeed, the benefits will flow. If you succeed only after a massive struggle, those benefits will be delayed and many a career will be bruised.

6. The Teamwork Exigency

You may be able to plan what your project team is going to do, but how do you plan what everyone else will do? You may have tight teams for FI-CO, SD, MM, and PP, but all of these teams also have to be as integrated as is SAP. One team, no matter how skilled and motivated, cannot be allowed to race too far ahead of the others. Your progress will tend to be measured by your slowest team and our ability to keep the others working in a lockstep.

Deadlines Are for News Reporters

Every project is assigned a deadline, i.e. a date upon which everything will be finished. The system will be 'in' or 'up and running' and no further time or costs will be needed.

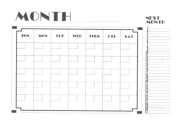

Management can look upon deadlines as expectation dates and the interim gestation periods as works-in-progress. But disappointments run rampant when it comes to deadlines, most especially when it comes to software implementations.

The facts are:

- Most systems implementations are late and over budget.

- All SAP implementations are late and over budget.

How can this be true? Are all systems personnel the world over lazy and incompetent? Is every project manager disorganized and blind? Can it be that difficult to bring an implementation in on time and on the money?

No. But setting a proper deadline is more guesswork than science and therein lies the key to terms like 'late' and 'over budget'.

Attitudes play a big part in this. Planning is largely the art of predicting the future, but plans are often bent out of shape by individual or collective surreality.

I was once the IS director for a large continuous printing firm and one of my important internal clients was the commercial director. He was the type of man who would hear that a salesman got a ten percent margin on a deal and would invariably remark that fifteen would have been better. His sales people learned to say that they got seven percent just to hear him say ten was the goal.

This man carried the same attitude when asking for IS services. I would offer him a delivery date and he would assume that I had dropped a time margin into my estimate. He was forever trying to chop three weeks down to two, or six months down to four. As far he was concerned, every job done for the commercial division of the company was 'late' and 'over budget.' My records showed us as more than 80% on target.

It is up to the project manager to establish a plan that allows for reality, not the expectations of upper management. And if the two cannot get together, that is, if upper management pressures the project manager to accelerate an implementation that should not be accelerated, the project is late and over budget the day it begins.

This is bad enough for a single application. It is nerve-wracking and close to tragic on an enterprise-wide SAP project. Management has to be supportive of the project even if it is 'late' and 'over budget' or the net effect is added stress to implementation teams, stress that is based upon a faulty conception of time rather than the ambitions of the business.

What happens to most SAP project plans:

1. Education (the learning curve) is not taken into account.

2. Previous projects are used as benchmarks, as in 'it only took five months to put the last financial package in.'

3. Upper management cannot believe the amount of consulting required and chops that portion of the budget.

4. Assumptions that in-house staff will be available for the project are 'optimistic.'

Crowning the plan is the deadline. September 1. January 1. April 30. These are favorites of most, and, in an SAP implementation, quite pointless.

In a hallway of a company where a ton of SAP work was being done was a poster with the slogan: "Success is Dream With a Deadline." Oh, really?

The assumption behind a deadline is that it whips people into line, as if without one they would dither and drift and leaf through the pages in the newspaper instead of getting to the grit of their jobs. The fact of the matter is that people do their jobs when they have direction and dignity. Deadlines erode dignity, while offering scant direction.

Some deadlines are natural, like payment terms, and have to be met. Others are management dementia. End of the year is one, though few systems outside of accounting systems demand such a deadline.

If there is a compelling business reason for a specific deadline, then you have to plan for the resources to meet that deadline, but you also have to be realistic. In many cases, you are already too late so trying to hit the deadline will only add anxiety throughout the entirety of the project.

At the onset of a major project that I managed in Tokyo, an IS manager asked me, through a translator, if we were going to set a deadline and on that day say we were finished, or were we going to do this the Japanese way and work as long as it would take to make a good system. He meant to be insulting, but he ended up being instructive. I had planned a deadline (which, it turned out, was wildly optimistic) but, after this conversation, I dropped it. This was in July of 1988 and I told the client that their system would be operational *in the spring of 1990.* March or April or May. There were numerous stresses throughout this project, but time wasn't one of them. We went live on May 30, 1990. Could we have done it faster? Of course, but at the cost of quality and the client would not have seen the same end benefit.

The moral of this story is that if deadlines have to be set, they should reflect the duration of the project and unless there are compelling business reasons, it is unwise to set rigid deadlines for SAP implementations.

Just for you, a handy guide:

DURATION	COMPLETION POINT
18 months or more	Spring, summer, winter, or fall
12 to 18 months	Any two months (e.g. April/May)
6 months	Any given month
Week	Friday or Saturday
Day	Anytime after lunch

Continuous Planning

An implementation plan for SAP should not be finalized at the beginning of a project and then left alone. It should be in continuous improvement right up to the final weeks of an implementation. Even if project scope is frozen at the outset, a multitude of other factors will render the initial plan useless before it is three months old. Among these:

1. Resources are seldom fully known at the beginning of a project; you do not know how good or bad your consultants are, or how much true SAP experience they possess, nor do you know how well your employees will 'adhere' to the project.

2. Outside education course schedules may not fit your plan.

3. Scope is never truly frozen, especially in an enterprise-wide undertaking.

4. You cannot possibly know everything that has to happen, most especially in the latter stages of the project.

Consider the various project planning levels:

Stage

Phase		Phase	
Activity	Activity	Activity	Activity
Task Task Task	Task Task Task	Task Task Task	Task Task Task

The classical three stages are Planning, Development, and Implementation. (For SAP projects, the Development Stage is viewed as Business Process Design/Configuration/Prototyping.)

Phases constitute the project outline, e.g. Establish the Vision, Form the Team, Install Hardware, End User Training, et al.

Activities are groups of tasks and tasks are the detail of what is done.

During the Planning Stage, it is not feasible to plan the Development Stage to any detail beyond Activity. In longer projects, the Implementation Stage should only be planned at Phase level.

In essence, Stage and Phase planning should be done for the entire project at the beginning. Activity planning can only be done at this point for the Planning and Development stages and, for development, not all activities can be taken into account. Activity planning can be done for the Implementation phase only when a major portion of development is completed. Task planning should only occur prior to the beginning of each phase.

You are strongly advised not to distribute a full blown project plan to everyone on the team at the beginning of a project. The amount of detail and the pages of tasks will confuse and overwhelm your staff, and they will be angry when you issue revised plans.

Instead, distribute a phase-level plan at the beginning of a project, with activity planning specific to each team for the first phases only and task planning only for the initial activities. As the project progresses, you will establish and distribute the detailed plans when they are needed, using the initial phased planning as a general team guideline.

The result will be that team members will have a clear view of the project direction and not be swamped with changing detail at task and activity level.

All the same, the initial plan must be clearly delineated from the outset. You have to come up with a viable budget and timeframe so that the project will have a direction and price tag. However, adding up the time and cost of pages upon pages of planned tasks is not going to result in a budget that makes sense. Begin with an aerial view, and as the project progresses, fly lower and the objectives and benefits will come into view.

The Just-in-Time Method of Consultant Planning

You should be counting on considerable involvement by your own staff, with every intention of having them lead the project to its completion. Still, you will certainly need some level of consulting to see you through.

You do not have to retain the same level of consultants from beginning to end during your project. All the same, finding the consultants you need when you need them for the duration of time that you need them can be difficult.

Good consultants are like Moses. They are given the opportunity to lead, but seldom see the Promised Land, the finish, the end zone. They parachute into your company, seek guidance in terms of what is expected of them, and hop to the beat of whatever music your firm can come up with. Good consultants force the beat into businesslike terms, and once the client is in good stead, disappear.

Here is a close-to-ideal curve of involvement between in-house staff and consulting staff for an SAP implementation.

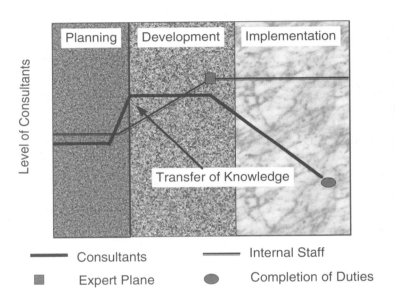

During the planning stage, you may well need a number of consultants to lend impetus and expertise to the strategic planning, team formation, and visioning. As this stage comes to an end, you would bring in the basic contingent of consultants needed to help you through the shoals of configuration and integration. It is best to have them show up before the first Monday in question, but not weeks in advance. Through the first two-thirds or so of the development stage, consultants will provide a transfer of SAP knowledge to your staff. They will provide impetus and expertise to the BPR and configuration activities while your staff is riding the learning curve.

Gradually, your staff will begin to take the reins away from the consultants. Configuration issues will no longer seem like Rubik cubes and your business processes will begin to make serious sense to all concerned. At this point, you will lessen the level of consultant presence in your company. You will have reached the Expert Plane (read on), and the benefits of your SAP implementation will swing into view.

Contingency Planning

I worked for some years for the City of St. Paul, Minnesota, and was not amused to find that by the end of each December, the budget for snow removal was already depleted. This was an annual issue because funds for snow removal were part of "contingency" and were spent in summer months as well as winter. The problem with this budget was that "contingency" was a catch-all rather than specific to an unpredictable variable (i.e. snowfall) and the result was emergency funding voted every January or February by the St. Paul City Council.

Contingency planning is the key to setting a proper plan and budget at the beginning without having to plan to task level. The measure of contingency that you apply will vary according to the measure of foreknowledge you have about each phase. Thus, there should not be a single amount of money or a single number of 'days' applied as contingency. Rather, each phase should have an element of contingency applied to allow for:

- planning assumptions that do not pan out

- your relative inexperience at the beginning of the project.

If you are allowing a 5% contingency for early phases, you might allow a 10% or even 15% contingency for the latter phases. If contingency for a given phase is not used, it should not be carried over to subsequent phases (unless you are in a terrible budget bind with upper management, in which case anything goes).

In setting contingencies, you are not creating 'fat', you are allowing for a margin of error. How you allow for this margin will play a major role in setting a realistic and conceivable project master plan.

A Planning Pyramid for SAP Projects

Much of this chapter deals with projects of all kinds. SAP projects have their peculiarities, however, and they must be addressed in planning.

- The learning curve.

- The natural resistance to change. In the case of SAP, the change is massive and the resistance can be mutually massive.

- The element of an enterprise-wide implementation means that planning will encompass the entire enterprise.

A number of our firm's consultants found themselves in an endless project in a southern city, where the resistance to SAP was on an enterprise-wide scale and management came up deuces when it was time to deal with that resistance. Old hands in the firm were referred to as We Be's as in "We be here before this SAP project and we be here when it's flushed down the john." As it happens, they *are* still there, and the project has been flushed down the john, in large part thanks to them.

This company did not plan on resistance. OK, that was only one of the mega-huge mistakes they made, but it was a costly one.

You must prepare for resistance, and plan on the time it takes to smooth it over. You must also be prepared for a steep learning curve, not only for your project staff but also for every employee affected by the project.

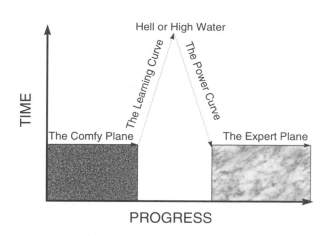

THE COMFY PLANE

The earliest phases of a project are a time for high-excitement and seemingly great strides. You develop the vision, form a team, create a budget and master plan, send a few key players off to SAP training courses, and fill the walls with charts. Consultants are getting to know where the restrooms are located and are honing their time-reporting skills. You have heard the phrase 'the key to success with SAP is (fill in the blank)' only thirty times or so, and the project manager is still going home before seven in the evening.

Ah, the comfy plane. Good meetings, pleasant lunches, nifty charts on the walls. The good life.

A tsunami is born a ripple. Any gust of Caribbean wind is a potential strand of a hurricane. A flake of snow lands on a mountain ledge and becomes part of an avalanche. So what's it going to be in your project? What innocuous, petty, annoying occurrence will lead you into  the difficulties of serious implementation? And how will you deal with it?

During the comfy plane, only the immediate project team and some of upper management are directly affected, and the balance of the company populace is still out of the loop. Ripples and gusts and a flake of snow.

THE LEARNING CURVE

Once configuration begins, the learning curve grows steep and daunting. What seemed, during the planning phases, like a row of hills, is revealed to be a full-scale mountain range. You are also on the slick slopes of BPR and having your first meetings with those who have heard about the project but have not been affected until NOW. The power curve is on the way, but first the highest peaks of the learning curve have yet to be viewed.

Now you are beginning to understand the complexity and the power of SAP. You are learning the configuration process and suddenly the principles begin to reveal themselves: integration and workflow. For the first time, you are aware of the depth of a system that includes over 8,000 tables, and those courses you took at SAP just have not prepared you.

If you only get serious about the learning curve while your company is already full of consultants, you will face two huge obstacles:

1. You are learning while the consultants (and you) are supposed to be progressing = this will be expensive

2. Those who are resisting the project for whatever reason will look upon it as a yawning chasm of costs and time and point to your apparent confusion as proof that SAP is not the solution.

How do you shorten the learning curve? You plan on it in advance, and make sure that a major portion of the hard learning is done before you reach this point in the project. You provide your key staff training to the practice and principles of configuration and integration. You educate management staff to SAP itself, what it is for and what it can do, and how it differs from classical systems implementation projects. In short, you do not arrive at this point with a perfect compass and an empty backpack.

THE POWER CURVE

As the learning curve is still on the rise, the power curve kicks in. Where these curves cross may decide the fate of your project. During the power curve, the company finds itself struggling with the feasibility of implementing SAP. Those who are riding the learning curve may be for it while those who are behind the curve will probably be resisting it. In the interim, the project bogs down. People with SAP knowledge have a hard time getting their ideas across to those who do not have SAP knowledge. Company traditions that are meant to be toppled by the project will be used as cannon by those who are bewildered by the goings-on.

It is during this period in the project that you sense you will never get there. Budgets and nerves are stretched thin and there's a whiff of overtime in the air.

If there has been management commitment from the outset, this curve is shortened. However, if management steps in only at this point, the project seems to be starting all over, with questions about cost and benefit being thrown around like paper airplanes. How long you have to put up with this curve is a function of the unity, management, and communications of your company, as well as by your preparation during the comfy plane.

The power curve ends when (or if?) there is a general consensus that SAP is still going to be implemented and those who have ridden the learning curve will lead that implementation.

THE EXPERT PLANE

It is at this point that you are ready to fly. You have had your training and your months of trial and error, and most of the political brushfires have been extinguished. Patience becomes more of an issue than before because you will have had months of indoctrination to SAP while end users and others are just having their baptism and these are the people who now become actively involved.

At this point, you are wearing the scars of implementation battle and you will begin to grow weary of debate. The temptation is to force your way to the end. Resist it. As the consultants made a transfer of knowledge to you, it is now for you to make a transfer of knowledge to those around you.

There Were Dinner Plans in Pompeii One Night

As you are planning, and revising the plan, you have to know that the project is not going to follow that plan line by line and point by point. Human nature and business events cannot be regimented by an MS Project file. Planning is all about forewarning and assumes, incorrectly, that you can predict the future with precision. If you see that the project is not following the plan, say so, loudly and in writing. Your co-workers and your management will appreciate the heads-up more than they would appreciate a sudden, last-minute disappointment.

Finally: the success of an SAP implementation is not measured by how closely that implementation stuck to the plan, but how fully your company realizes the intended benefits of the implementation. If plans change in order to bring benefit to the company, so much the better.

Orchestrate to benefit, not to deadline, and the tsunami will remain a ripple. Or, at worst, a drenching.

From Wanderer to Pathfinder

The Various Waves of an SAP Education

Education, Not Training Alone

Find in your career those memorable and lasting learning moments. How many of them took place in a classroom or auditorium? How many in your boss' office? How many over lunch with a pen and a notepad and a bottle of beer? And how many of them took place in the bitter field of business battle?

> Information is data endowed with relevance and purpose. Converting data into information requires knowledge.
>
> Peter Drucker
> Harvard Business Review
> January/February 1988

What moments in your business life do you ponder late at night, when facing the movie screen of your bedroom ceiling? What is it in your career that ruins your sleep?

Failure. Or, at best, the struggle.

It is clear that we learn more from our failures than from our successes. When we make decisions that lead to disastrous results, we tend to carry the bruises of those results for years. We analyze and replay what went wrong, and in that analysis comes the lesson. When we succeed, the analysis is less intense. Failures are scrutinized as abnormal, victories dismissed as routine.

But victories, in the SAP world or elsewhere, are not routine. Take stock of the last ten initiatives in your own company and you will find that roughly one third yielded expected results. Of late, SAP has been under fire for the length, complexity, and cost of implementation. It is true that in the world of SAP implementations, there is a killing field of education, scrolls of regret and what if and why and maybe. SAP implementations embrace entire enterprises and their near and mid-term destinies. The stakes are high, higher than most players are prepared to believe.

When we look into the causes behind difficult implementations, we generally find miniscule education budgets. We also find that upper management knows very little about SAP beyond the contents and tag lines of brochures. Not surprisingly, upper management usually has high expectations of what SAP will do for their company.

Chris Carlsen reminds all of us frequently that SAP requires an education—and not merely training—because *one must acquire knowledge* through a systematic and systemic understanding of SAP concepts. Training is the learning of skills through apprenticeship and practice. Skills training is a piece of the puzzle in developing our concept of an SAP education; yet skills training alone is not sufficient for your company's successful implementation of SAP. I may revert to the standardized use of the word "training" from time to time, but please focus on the concept of acquiring knowledge with an education in SAP.

Our conclusions, based upon numerous experiences and observations, are that SAP implementation failures are due primarily to a lack of upfront knowledge of what SAP is and is not prior to the signing of a license. Further, that lack of upfront knowledge is too seldom bridged in the early stages of a project. It is only after months of effort that most firms get the point, stop the project, go back to square one to educate themselves, and then begin again. Check out the SAP success stories and you will find that most of them have this start, stop, learn, start again cycle in their history.

You can avoid the cost and heartbreak of this cycle by investing in education now. Learn or perish. ASAP.

Ready, Fire, Aim!

There are a sufficient number of cadavers on the battlefield for post-mortems galore. SAP implementation failures are as common as dandelions and their seeds tend to land in articles in 'Computer World' and 'Information Weekly'. You can hear the low mooing from sea to shining sea and if you are fast on the uptake, you have already discerned that the 'victims' claim that SAP itself was at fault.

The more immediate fault lies in an attitude of instant gratification, in which companies seek to implement SAP by jamming it down the throats of their employees. And the fastest, cheapest, and most short-sighted way of doing this is to leap straight from installation to configuration. Configuration tasks are the 'firing' tasks, the unleashing of decision arrows to hit strategic targets. Too few companies settle on aiming until after configuration has missed a thousand such targets. Most of us have had similar experiences on a much smaller scale. We have ordered software for our laptops or desktops, installed the software with a quick Run a:\setup and then endeavored to use it without so much as glancing at the user manual. Installation is rapid, mastery is much slower. Our next hundred steps are accompanied by furious flipping of pages between the index and whatever text we can (hurriedly) absorb to speed us on our way. In essence, we muddle for a stretch, then become novices and, only after long manipulation, do we master the game.

Multiply this North American tic that is a part of us by the number of people in your company who will be relied upon to make SAP work. Throw in a square or a cube multiplier. Add social and career stress. Let simmer three to six months. Smell the burning.

Back to the Future

Most of your staff will have already lived through the implementation of more than one information system prior to your choice of SAP. But SAP implementations are different and you will not be prepared for them just because you've already implemented other systems.

Your people need to be prepared, but most companies dive right into an implementation project with little upfront education beyond SAP training for key players and the odd seminar. You would not hire high school graduates to be managers in your company, but by pressing your management staff into service in SAP implementations, you are sending that staff back to the future because the  management and business skills that have been learned and practiced in the past are easily confused by this hybrid business process-IT solution. An assumed IT approach is a fatal mistake. The tasks and activities that management once performed when implementing classic information systems no longer fully apply.

What is so different? Up till now, your staff has dealt with information systems as a service to be provided by IS or IT or whatever you call it in your firm. Business people have asked for services and been required to define their needs in functional specifications. IS staff has interpreted those specifications and fulfilled them through a combination of software acquisition and programming, and the programming has not been accomplished by the business staff.

In SAP, programming is not the issue. Configuring is the issue. Programming is the creation of *codes* that direct the order, path, disposition, and destination of information. Configuring is the setting

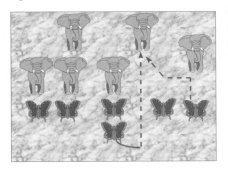 of *business tables* that direct the order, path, disposition, and destination of information. Programming is a mechanical function. Configuration is a business function.

Show a business manager this phrase and see what he or she does with it:

SET VAR TO 4 GO CHAIN TO RT 742
RETURN IF 3 PAUSE
WRITE TO CALL

Programming creates a distance between business and its satisfaction. This distance has been extant since the beginning of data processing.

Business may have called the tune, but IS has played all the instruments. SAP bridges that distance in a revolutionary fashion by bringing language back to business.

When we are kids playing football, we call plays like 'Patty go deep and, Chris, you better block that fat guy.' By the time you get even as far as high school, the same play is referred to as 'X Post right, Cross 4, Center slam.' In high school, eleven players need to be given detailed direction in a terse, quick fashion, so plain directions are turned into a lingual program. 'X Post right' describes the route the wide receiver will run, 'cross 4' tells the running back to fake a run around the right tackle, and 'center slam' means all the linemen better block that fat guy.

In the same fashion, old-style programming turned your functional requirements into code and then shipped back to you an approximation of what you had asked for.

In SAP implementations, the code is behind the curtain and plain business language has been restored to you. Instead of specifying to IS what you want, you are able to specify for yourselves, in business language, through configuration. When you configure SAP according to a business process design, you are placing values on data fields with headings you understand like 'Order Verification Limit' or 'Maximum Quantity Allowed'. You may determine which fields do or do not appear on a given screen. You may decide how multi-currency accounting will occur (with a daily EDI update of rates or through manual entry on a weekly basis, or whatever). And you are doing this with the minimal intervention of programmers, who should only be patching the functions of SAP that do not satisfy your deepest business cravings.

And if your management asks you to do this without prior education to SAP, you are running the thorn fields with no pants and your implementation project will become a bewildering and anxiety-ridden undertaking.

The activity of sitting in a paper-filled conference room for hours with IS managers is not new to most of your staff. They may be well versed in how to define their needs and may even be pretty sharp at following up through the implementation of a single application.

But they do not know how to configure SAP, as a team, into a seamless workflow-oriented applications suite. Asking them to take on this task without sufficient prior SAP education is like sending them back to high school level, hiring them straight from the prom, and putting them squarely onto the deck of your ship in the midst of a major sea battle.

They will probably sink, as might your ship.

However, if you have provided sufficient training, you will:

- reduce the need of outside consultants in a big way;

- motivate your staff by virtue of the investment you have made in their skills (and the consequent trust you are placing in them);

- create a pool of in-house SAP expertise that is already knowledgeable in the ways of your company, thus reducing the time required for the dreaded AS IS phase (more on this subject is yet to come);

- acquire a basis of understanding that will lead to credible planning and budgeting of the project;

- provide a basis for a proper management of expectations (i.e. what SAP will or will not do for your company);

- identify those who can make the leap and those who cannot.

SAP training pays off better than does SAP consulting.

A Case Study in Mastering Your Direction

I am not a devout believer in Japanese business methods. On the contrary, I am a devout skeptic of many of the business practices that were all the rage in the 1980s, a time in which the presumption was that Japanese methods were the key to their (currently lagging) success. All the same, I learned many lessons from my one project in that country, and wish to pass on one of these lessons in this context.

During a two-year project, I ran a team of Englishmen from Coopers & Lybrand who had already distinguished themselves in a number of projects throughout Europe. Based on previous successes, we were chosen to solve a serious problem for the same firm in Japan. In the latter stages of the project (pre-SAP) I planned on a three-month handover of our design to a third-party Japanese programming outfit. I planned on a five-month programming phase, with implementation to occur at the end of this period.

The design handover was complicated by language, of course, and I had thought myself wise to have added one month more than I might have under usual circumstances. But after the first two months of design handover had been spent, my team was telling me that we would be going over budget. The Japanese programming firm was adding more and more meetings, many of them (to our thinking) redundant. One meeting with three programmers would be followed by another with the same three programmers and two more. Yet another meeting would include a mix of those from the first two and perhaps one or two new people.

I grasped for an English-Japanese lexicon to look up the word 'stress.'

The design handover phase took altogether five months, two beyond my project plan. But the programming took only three, two less than my project plan. The implementation came in on time. I grasped for my English-Japanese lexicon to look up the word for 'how the hell did that happen?'

The lexicon's answer: the third-party Japanese programming firm did not want design handover from designer to programming team leader, but to all of the programmers, again and again, until such time as every member of the team had master the design from head to toe. Once that was accomplished, programming was a race to the finish, without the customary 'Jeremy, I'm a bit in the dark about those dodgy inventory routines. Diabolical, what. Can we arrange a meeting?'

The team mastered the direction before racing to it with full confidence. Given the sweat and stress of my lone venture into a project in Japan, I have often thought, 'Never again.' However, I admit to feeling curious about an SAP implementation managed in just such a fashion.

The team mastered the direction before racing to it with full confidence.

And they were on time and on budget. There's a concept.

An Inventory of Required Education

You have already read a number of articles that describe the massive rise in training budgets, corporate re-education, orientation, or whatever sobriquet is given to learning in the business place. In the 1970s, it was assumed that job skills had to be re-learned every six years or so. Ding dong, it is 1997 and new job skills have to be learned every week. This is not necessarily a bad phase in the workaday world. It is, at worst, reality, and, at best, evolution. The fact that you are reading this book instead of the latest attorney-saves-the-day potboiler is proof that we are all in the same bind. So, let's make the most of what we have here.

Now that your company is in an SAP frame of mind, acceleration of learning must become the rhythm of activity. On the one hand, you have the daily business to take care of and on the other hand, you are now being asked to change the shape of your business face so that you can look into an SAP mirror. You and your cohorts will succeed, I promise you, if you insist upon, and obtain, proper training and education to SAP prior to undertaking the massive scope of an SAP do dah.

It would be far too simplistic to assume that you and your staff need SAP education. All the same, this is the assumption that most companies plop into their budgets at the onset of such a project. What is truly needed is a more horizontal look at the training required, who needs it, and when.

The education levels to be addressed in your company are as follows:

- Management
- Implementation team
- IS support staff
- End users

- New job training (resulting from BPR)
- Peripheral skills (Windows, PC skills)
- Preparing the company for change

SAP Education for Management

We are constantly finding situations where upper management is at the end of a collective rope because of the 'delays' and 'cost overruns' of an SAP implementation, and we are no longer surprised by the dismay of vice presidents who complain about the high cost and slow progress of their SAP projects. When we dig into the causes of the cost and the 'slow' progress, we invariably find that management has only a vague clue as to what the SAP implementation project was intended to fulfill. What does surprise us is the number of companies that are deep into implementation, in trouble, and on the ropes, and the company management is still at square one, and the head-scratching is a percussive beat.

Management tends to assume that SAP implementations are similar to other implementations of software that have already been undertaken by the company since the early seventies. This is the worst and most damaging fallacy of any such endeavor because it fosters misguided expectations in terms of time, budget, and intended benefits. The stroke of a pen over a software license is no big deal when the subject is a new financial system. Techies and bean-counters alone can install such a system, with only a minimum of shrieking and cost over-runs.

SAP itself offers an overview course. SAP also offers a number of video-guided slide shows. What SAP doesn't offer is a detailed look at who you are before you stain that license with a signature. It is not in their interest to do more than they do. You are the buyer, they are the seller. Therefore, consider this, you CEO, and you COO, and you CIO. You are contemplating an investment in the millions of dollars, an investment that will pit your company's fate against your company's ability to succeed in this project. You intend to launch your company into the next milennium and you are wildly attracted by the most magnificent enabler of business leap-frog of all time. Will you seek guidance with SAP or with the Big 6 partners? OK. Nice touch. Little steps for little feet. Or will you pour yourself into more learning?

Seek out a seminar, a second, a third. Do this before committing much more money. Send a few trusted lieutenants to other seminars. Compare notes. Spend $23.95 on a book that will give you a head start. Or spent another $23.95 on yet another book. Your time alone is worth ten times the price of these books, and what you learn will save your company untold thousands.

For this education alone, you may spend overall $100K of your firm's money on seminars and another $100K on trusty consultants. If you are looking at a $20 million or $50 million company investment, these amounts will pale, and will be absorbed, provided you are in search of a serious and attainable return on investment.

The benefits of management SAP training are vast:

- realistic project plans and budgets can be drawn, thus radically reducing stress within the implementation team

- return on investment will almost certainly become the centerpiece of the project, as it should be

- expectations will be settled at the onset and there will be a great reduction of finger-pointing

- management will be in a position to adequately assess outside consultants, their readiness, and their performance.

A last consideration on this score: if SAP training is provided to middle management staff and below, upper management is not going to remain in a position to lead the company once SAP is implemented.

SAP Education for Your Implementation Team

You will assemble your best and your brightest and attempt to mold them into a team. Early on, you may be dependent upon outside consultants to drive your project, but you do not want this situation to last forever.

It is probable that a number of your implementation team members are middle managers, whose previous positions will be eliminated as a result of this project. You may look upon these people as your in-house support not only throughout the implementation period, but beyond the implementation, when your company will continue to adjust and configure SAP to continually improve and bring ever more benefit to your enterprise.

What you are attempting is to create a pool of internal SAP consultants who can take the expensive torch away from external consultants and help you race to an implementation victory while that torch is still lit.

The following chart describes what we consider the path that your people should follow:

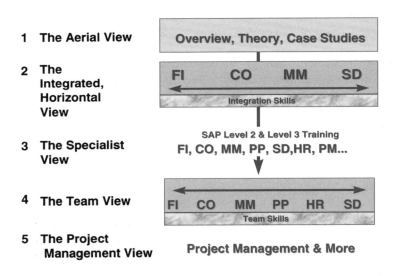

1	**The Aerial View**	**Overview, Theory, Case Studies**
2	**The Integrated, Horizontal View**	**FI CO MM SD** — Integration Skills
3	**The Specialist View**	SAP Level 2 & Level 3 Training — FI, CO, MM, PP, SD,HR, PM...
4	**The Team View**	**FI CO MM PP HR SD** — Team Skills
5	**The Project Management View**	**Project Management & More**

PHASE ONE: THE AERIAL VIEW

SAP offers product training, which can be viewed as the classical (vertical) training. Anyone needing in-depth education to Sales & Distribution can attend SAP's overview course, then its levels 1 through 3 courses and attain a fully rounded SD education. This alone will not sufficiently qualify someone to effectively participate in what will prove to be a horizontal, workflow-oriented implementation.

Instead, potential implementation team members should first be schooled in the business basics of SAP. The SAP overview course will be helpful, but it will be limited to SAP itself and will not cover all of the peripheral issues of an implementation, such as:

- what is so different about SAP?

- what are the implementation issues?

- how much business process reengineering is required to make it work?

- while we are at it, what *is* business process reengineering?

- what role can consultants play in the project?

- who will do what and how will they do it?

Many of these and other questions are addressed in our first book, *In the Path of the Whirlwind, An Apprentice Guide to the World of SAP*. Many other issues are addressed in this book. But more background should be provided, including case study laboratories and implementation scenarios because no two SAP implementation projects are identical and there is no recipe, no fat-pages-in-multiple-binder methodologies, no linear step-by-step guidebook in existence.

Therefore, a first phase of orientation and positioning is required, and you should not shortchange yourselves in this regard. If you leap into direct SAP product training, you will emerge with more questions than answers. Questions cost money and time. Answers reduce spending and time. This is an investment with a clear return.

PHASE TWO: THE INTEGRATED HORIZONTAL VIEW

We cannot help but repeat ourselves. The facts of SAP life tend to loop back to each other in this very redundant fashion. SAP is an integrated suite of applications that leads you to learn and apply workflow as opposed to vertical applications that are scotch-taped (i.e. interfaced) to each other and hanging by a costly thread. Therefore, your implementation team has to learn the tenets of integration as quickly and as fully as possible. Integration can and should be learned in tandem with the nuts and bolts of configuration.

It is not enough for someone tabbed to configure the Financials (FI) of SAP to simply learn FI because the causes of configuration decisions for FI will have effects on the configuration of SD, MM, PP, and the rest. Thus, the second phase of education should be a solid grounding in configuration principles with an accent on integration points.

One of the most effective training *experiences* will be the creation of a test company, including the configuring and integration of the key modules: FI, CO, SD, and MM. Hands-on education is a must at this point. Lecture and reading will be of limited value.

PHASE THREE: THE SPECIALIST VIEW

There are no Renaissance men or women in the world of SAP. The entirety of SAP cannot and has not been mastered by any one person. The sheer vastness and depth of SAP (as in business itself) makes us all specialists in one way or another. For example, this book has largely been crafted by a specialist in the arena of project management who is incapable of configuring the MM module but might have a clue or two about FI.

Your staff will necessarily end up with specialist labels: FI, SD, MM, PP. It's the way of the SAP world to slot people into one or another of these. Experienced consultants, and occasionally internal staff, often gravitate toward the hyphenates, such as SD-MM, FI-CO, or MM-PP because of the horizontal and integrated nature of SAP.

At this point, however, you must allow your people to school themselves in their specific subjects. Now you will send them to SAP level 2 and 3 training where they can concentrate on the key and direct aspects of the modules for which they will be directly responsible.

SAP America provides these courses, on a very regular basis, in half a dozen cities.

PHASE FOUR: PROJECT TEAM EDUCATION

The vast majority of SAP implementation projects have a room somewhere, often referred to as the 'War Room' (sigh) in which implementation team members work together, elbow to elbow, for weeks on end, configuring and process designing and re-configuring until the SAP model meets general satisfaction in a prototype.

What happens more often than not is that these team members are first separate, each working (fruitlessly) in a vertical fashion, which is traditional, but they then tend to move closer and closer to each other, out of necessity, to make things work properly. The duration from project launch to the time they all show up in a 'War Room' (sigh again) can be weeks or months depending upon their collective antennae and the quality of your project management.

What we are recommending here is a mid-level education phase in which these people are thrown together into a two-week team training exercise during which their team and SAP skills will be tested and refined in parallel.

Some team members may fall by the wayside during such training. Or you may find that the roles that you have projected for some members would best be adjusted. The cost of such

lessons is minor compared to the costs that will be assumed once the project is live. This phase of the training will verify that your team can be just that, a team.

A final note: just for the sake of diversity, name the room in which you all meet something other than the War Room. Try the Peace and Harmony Room, or the United Nations, or the Filthy Rich if This Works Room. Something upbeat, at any rate, some name that will not bespeak of bloodletting.

What Kind of Team Are You Seeking?

A football team works together as a collection of specialists under the firm control of a coach. This may be a preferable team for an SAP implementation. Another approach is to create a team comparable to a tennis doubles team in which each player's strength can be used to advantage and each player's weakness can be compensated or covered by another player's strengths. Such a team will require less coaching (management) and provide sufficient leeway for creativity and impetus.

PHASE FIVE: THE PROJECT MANAGEMENT VIEW

This education is not for everyone involved in the implementation, but should be made available to project managers, directors, and team leaders. The fact that you are reading this book puts you into the project management view. It is admittedly unclear as to what additional education you may need to be prepared to head up an SAP implementation. Even if you have already successfully managed other large implementations, you will need more education to understand the integration of SAP as well as the demands of managing a team which requires closer cooperation than what may have been required for your other projects. What is essential is to avoid relying overmuch on past IS development-implementation experience and maintain an open view in regard to an SAP implementation.

If you are a project manager, you need to know that your main role is not coordination of resources, it is leadership. The scrambling of career paths in your wake (you are, of course, the living, breathing symbol of the project to all who cross your path) will be the most prominent problem to be addressed. You should be prepared to reach for help and guidance in areas that are beyond your range. Change management springs to mind, as do network, client/server issues.

The trusty old 'cult of personality' method that could work in classical software implementations will be a creaky failure in SAP implementations because of the sheer and undeniable scope of the project. A project manager must be prepared to learn and one of the most important lessons is to learn delegation and assignment of peripheral key issues. Another lesson is to respect that fact that everyone around you is, at least for a time, an apprentice to all that is happening. Further, the apprentice of all subjects is the project manager, who can only delve into second or third levels of subjects that reach into far greater depths.

Business seems simple and an SAP project can help all concerned to bring simplicity to the surface. But it is a fact that no one can master all facets of business and, by extension, no one can master all facets of SAP.

SAP Implementation Team Education - A Bargain However You Look at It

The cost of an SAP education for your implementation team will be in the neighborhood of $10-20K per person. If this seems steep to you, take a look at:

- your potential consulting tab, with rates of $150 per hour and up

- the ROI you are aiming for

- the risk you are taking in doing this project.

If you spend $15K for a team member, this is the equivalent of 100 hours of outside consulting or 2 ½ weeks of Mr. or Ms. *Experienced* SAP Consultant. You can assume a solid ROI within the first three to four months of your project and diminishing consulting costs throughout the duration of the project. Further, your risk is reduced by virtue of having created in-house expertise rather than maintaining a continued reliance on outside help.

Your overall education costs may well reach 15% to 20% of your entire implementation costs, and you will certainly lose a great shank of this investment when the people you have conscientiously trained leave your firm for high-paying positions in the world of SAP consulting. Refer to our chapter dedicated to consulting for tips on how to hang onto your internal consultants.

SAP Education for IS Support

In launching an SAP project, you may be facing a surly crew of internal IS staff. If the project succeeds, those legacy systems that have long been their bread and butter will be no more, so why would they support you in this endeavor?

Many of your IS people will read the handwriting on the wall and disappear well before you wish them to. Others will read that same handwriting in a more positive way and sign on for re-training into the world of SAP. These are your nuggets and you must address their training needs early on, or they may follow the others out the door and you will find yourself with a technical vacuum that will pose untold problems.

There are multiple areas of education that need to be covered and there is no single line of training that can be outlined here. Despite the open systems architecture offered by SAP, it is a fact that BASIS operations tend to be somewhat hardware specific. If your hardware park is largely Hewlett Packard, training should be skewed toward UNIX. If you are using the Oracle database, there will be training required in that arena.

You will almost certainly need someone with solid systems administration background. The velocity and impact of SAP upgrades alone will require this. If you count on SAP to provide assistance each time an upgrade is to be accomplished, you will be in a vulnerable position both technically and financially.

At the same time, as your IS staff is converted to SAP, there are some serious, cost-related cautions:

1. In classical systems, programming has provided the solution to business needs and classical IS staff is probably program-oriented. If you take a pool of C+ programmers and teach them ABAP, they will assume that their new charge in life is to write ABAP programs in response to user-group requests. You do not want outlaw ABAP programming to filter into your SAP establishment. If you allow this, upgrades will be costly if not unfeasible and system maintenance will revert to the same nightmare that you have had with classical systems.

2. IS has until this point been in the forefront of 'technical solutions to business problems' and the cultural change to 'business solutions for business problems' may take time. Moving IS from the driver's seat to the passenger seat (i.e. in a navigational position at best, and a mechanic position in reality) will require more than SAP technical training.

Entirely new technical skills will be required of your remaining IS staff. Electronic Data Interchange and the Internet are currently in the forefront of what you need to address. (Hang on for SAP 3.1!) A thousand years ago, a key business issue was currency. Did you client pay in gold or mud? A hundred years ago, the first serious workflow subjects reared their heads. SAP can cover multi-currency issues such as gold or mud. Workflow is central to SAP. *Connectivity* is the issue of the beginning of this next millenium and if you fail to stress this aspect on the IS (or IT) side, you will lose major benefits that SAP is intended to afford, not only in 1997-98, but well beyond.

Business Process Reengineering

Beyond the softness of Quality Circles and the consequent and temporary repercussions of Total Quality Management, there has arisen a business wave and attitude given the label BPR or Business Process Reengineering.

SAP and BPR have been viewed as synonymous from the onset of the announcement of R/3 in late 1992. Both the product of SAP and the theory of BPR have been put into play to a high degree in the interim, with mixed results. The theory is that if you can rationally reengineer your business, you will need an infrastructural support for that reengineered business and the most apt support in existence is SAP R/3. We buy into this theory, wholly.

Business systems and methods, developed since the 50s and refined through subsequent decades, have tended toward a continued compartmentalization of skills. In the 1980s, new and improved business methods were introduced by theorists and put into premature practice throughout the world and especially North America, eager as it was to 'catch up' with Japan. At this writing, the 'catching up' is a moot point. The global economy is riding a flatter treadmill and a smoother treadmill, and the heat over Japanese management and distribution techniques is no longer a hot button board-room issue. The new hot button is reengineering and this is a subject that we cannot and will not belabor here, given a lack of space. Let it suffice to re-use a simple phrase that is often seen pinned to cubicle walls, a slogan worth practicing: DO NOT WORK HARDER, WORK SMARTER.

Work is at the core of BPR, the measure and flow and direction of work. And the work to be designed and charted must be work that drives toward profit and client satisfaction, and must therefore be based upon a desire to cut to the chase. You will be in need of people who are of a mood to discuss this simple principle, separate from company tradition, political maneuvering, or individual turf. These people will also need a star to follow, a vision, if they are to come up with tangible, feasible high level charts of processes that can be the basis for SAP configuration.

What education can be afforded to those among you who will be entrusted with the task of reengineering your corporation? SAP is not the issue here. As you form your team, each member must know SAP as a series of bridges and uprights and tubes and joints that will support whatever design you decide to adopt. SAP is not business, it is business support. BPR is your business plan; therefore, whoever makes the plan had better be a star, or better a group of stars, in your midst.

We have not yet answered the question as to the training these people should have. First and foremost, they should have a solid grounding, with experience, in the basic tenets of the business you are doing and intend to do over the coming years. What are you making or doing, who buys what you make or do, and why will they go on buying what you make or do?

Have the team in question read the basic books on reengineering and have them attend a few seminars in SAP. If their first attempts result in fat binders of box-arrow-box charts, they have misunderstood the ends and means of the exercise. If their output points directly address benefits like faster order turnaround to the tune of 200%, you will have a team ready to do business.

If upper management leaves BPR as an assignment to some far-flung team, or, worse, to outside consultants, the results will be spotty. My favorite phrase from the masterwork, *Reengineering the Corporation*, by Michael Hammer and James Champy is: *you are not rearranging the deck chairs on the Titanic.* Cut this out. Pin it to your receptionist's lapel. He will wear it with a certain dubious pride and you will be reminded each time you pass him on your way to the restroom.

Here is where we cut bait. Business process reengineering is the primary issue of what you are doing; SAP will support your BPR, not the other way around. This book, alone, will not suffice for BPR. Read further, and prosper.

New Processes, and Then What?

Will this chapter ever end? More education?

Now that you have re-arranged the deck chairs on the Titanic, everyone has to move places, don't they? There are new business processes involved, new horizons abounding, and new everything.

At least now we dig back to the SAP implementation. As BPR moves to configuration, scripting occurs. A script is exactly what you think it is, a listing of what each player does to make an action occur in an event-process chain, or EPC as SAP likes to put it. I receive an order (an event) and I enter the order to the system (a process), and once that order hits the system, all kinds of things happen (events) that lead to other processes until the order is filled and the cash is collected.

We are by now light years past BPR and configuration. We have reached the 'end user', as the phrase goes. The end user is he/she who pushes keys on a keyboard or runs a bar code reader over the bumper of a tractor-trailer and then fills out a form that will be entered (via keyboard) into the system.

At the core, end user training tends to settle into keystrokes, barcode sweeps, and the occasional filling out of comments fields. In a wider sense, it has to do with new empowerments and responsibilities.

Prior to SAP, those who filled in boxes in forms or keyed in data were doing so for their compartmentalized functions. Jonesy on the loading dock clicked his Bic to check off his receipt of six boxes of stuff, scrolled his initials onto a carboned form, and bit into his sandwich. One carbon went to accounting, another to the stock room, and the sandwich was ok, but why did they forget the mayo again?

In Jonesy's new world, that click is not a pen, it is a keyboard, a light pen, or a bar code. That sweep of a hand and that signature will kick data right into accounting, materials management, and probably sales and distribution. So the end user training has become corporate awareness in one stroke. It is time to teach Jonesy more than how to use a pen.

With a simple stroke of basic training, Jonesy is the equivalent of what once was a manager.

So? Give Jonesy and yourself the benefit of some serious dialog and some training.

End User Training

This is usually the only training that is budgeted, the simple training of those who will use the key strokes that move the data from one file to another. Whole projects tend to sink or swim on this training, when, in reality, it should be nothing more than a raw asterisk to all that has preceded this phase of events.

In simple terms, the scripting of new processes that led to configuration should allow the creation of end user training material. Show anyone a script to follow and the end result is comprehension.

A number of companies turn this phase over to third party specialist firms, end user trainers. Mmmmm. Why?

Third party end user trainers are experts in

1. gathering the thrust of your efforts

2. funneling scripts into basic functions

3. documenting functions into user guides

4. teaching end users the basic functions.

The problem we have with this practice is that the people who designed and configured the business flows are taken out of the equation. Alice will pipe up, in the midst of some training session, with several tart but salient questions that third party end user trainers will not have a chance of answering. So we can shoot Alice or we can revert to sanity and let the same group that built the temple explicate how to move from the steps to the altar. But only if we let these golden people learn the dance steps.

New Job Training

This happens. You are going to be faced with a whole field, whole tribes of people that you need in your company whose jobs have been altered or re-directed. What do you plan for them?

Above and beyond training for whatever they are now expected to do, there are peripheral skills to be considered. Do they do Windows, for example? Do they know Windows 95 or Windows 97? Can they handle pull down menus? Do they know how to connect one non-SAP function into the mainstream of all that you are building?

Of course they don't. Train them.

Preparing the Company for Change

If I had called this section *Change Management*, it it likely that the corners of your mouth would have curled. You would probably be snickering or already considering flipping ahead to the next section. The mere mention of change management tends to send management level folks into a deep swoon. Eyes roll, wallets are clenched, and laughter is in the works.

The feeling is that change cannot be managed and change management courses and consulting have been deemed as far too soft, too generic, and not bottom-line oriented.

Some months ago I was invited to meet a vice president of a huge company that was attempting to implement SAP and was in the throes of a magnificent failure. The vice president had read our first book and was something of a fan and accorded me a fairly royal welcome. As coffee was being served, I proceeded to breeze through a rapid introduction of myself, our company, and the SAP consulting and education services we provide. As I concluded, the vice president leaned back, smiled, and remarked, "So, you're not going to sell me any of that change management snake oil."

My response was a garbled and inchoate denial mixed with a garbled and inchoate rejoinder that change management, all the same, would be a must for this man's company. I have spent many hours scratching my head to figure out what it was that put me into such a state and have come to a number of conclusions:

1. Change management is a child of the 1980's wave of gizmo consulting products in which the major product lead was perceived, often rightfully so, as touchy feely.

2. TQM, quality circles, and the like were perceived as failures and may well have been in the context of management expectations of what they would provide companies.

3. All the same, any company that underwent the agonies of such projects, failure notwithstanding, at least put their employees into a evolutionary mode that prepared them for revolutionary activities such as SAP implementations.

Today, change management has matured and should not be such an object of derision. Business concepts tend to mature according to the marketplace and its perception and appreciation (read: bottom line) of those ideas. It has been a while since we have come upon sales teams that prepare themselves by climbing mountains together, or white-water rafting together to prove teaming skills. Those that did so in the 1980s got cold and wet. The 90s have provided both a towel and some focus.

We like to emphasize the concept of *preparing the company for change.* Your company needs to focus on providing awareness of the difficulties and struggles which people undergo at all levels of the company. In essence, *preparing the company for change focuses on the human side* of your SAP implementation effort:

- smoothing over resistance to change

- facilitating job conversion

- addressing 'survival guilt' in a downsized environment

- the other education already discussed in this chapter; if you are training your staff, you are already sending a positive signal.

We repeatedly stress in this book that SAP implementations are not pretty or humane. They are characterized by high anxiety, excessive hours of work, occasional anger, and the fog of wonder. Companies do not undergo such projects with individual needs in mind, nor even the collective. Money and survival and growth are the reasons behind an SAP implementation and its usual accompaniments of BPR and/or downsizing. Waves like these lead to confusion and anger and resistance. The bottom line is that you can train employees to follow the directions but if you fail to address their natural confusion and resistance to change, you are reducing them to the level of company tools.

If your company has 1,000 employees and you are spending $10 or $20 or $30 million on this project, you would be well advised to add another million or so to *prepare your company for change.* You will

94

still have to pick and choose among the companies that offer help in this arena, but you still should pick one or another.

A final note: we are still in close contact with this vice president, and he is now a firm believer in these same principles, having bruised himself badly when trying to implement SAP without having taken change management into account.

This is sand, this SAP, and we can lift a palmful and many grains will run out between our fingers. Those that remain are our acquired knowledge and experience. So we run our hands back into the sand, again and again. And there will always be more sand. Our only hope is to educate ourselves, or to pray for bigger hands.

The next book in THE CONSULTING ALLIANCE'S series on SAP— *People in the Whirlwind: The Human Side of an SAP Implementation—* will concentrate on preparing your company for change.

The Best Use of Scouts and Mercenaries

Getting the Most out of your Consultants

Why You Will Have Consultants, One Way or Another

If you have ever tried to repair a car yourself and then given up and taken it into a garage, you will most certainly have noted that Roy and Al are shaking their heads and smiling to each other. One of them will have the nerve to say that you should have come to them in the first place.

A few days later, you will drive your newly-humming car out of the garage and into the rest of your life. Roy and Al will have repaired it, and you will pay the bill, but you will not have learned what Roy and Al did to repair the car. And if it breaks down again, you will go back to them, and they may make the very same repairs, and send you the very same bill.

It should not be this way with SAP consultants. You will need them, yes, but you should not need them forever. If Roy and Al are SAP consultants, they will not only be building your system for you; they will be teaching you how to build it for yourself. And once you've got the hang of it, Roy and Al can retire to the Caribbean but they won't be billing you any longer.

The point is: you need an infusion of expertise that should be limited to a) a boost and b) a transfer of knowledge.

Even if you strip your company of all of its best people and apply them 100% to the project, you will not succeed without some help from the outside. You may have read elsewhere about companies that have traveled the SAP route with a minimum of consulting help. Read carefully and you will note that these companies did one or both of the following:

- implemented a very limited number of modules, such as FI and SD

- invested in SAP training in a big way.

Disrupting your current business is riskier and costlier than having consultants give you a leg up in the first few phases of an SAP implementation. What you are looking for is a balance between evolution and interruption. A simple tip: interrupting short term events is less costly and less important than you think.

The Rare, The Elusive, and the Expensive

SAP exploded on the North American scene in 1993 when R/3 was announced. In this same year, Hammer and Champy's book *Reengineering The Corporation* created a corporate firestorm. Reengineering cannot succeed without proper systems support to enable it, and SAP was clearly viewed as the most desirable enabler. Vast numbers of Fortune 500 companies rushed to license SAP and then looked around to find there was almost no one on the continent with SAP experience.

Four years have passed and the demand for experienced SAP help has continued to exceed the supply. Consultants with less than a year of experience go for $150 an hour or more and the level of client dissatisfaction has risen each year.

It is estimated that in 1997, the demand for SAP consultants will exceed 20,000. This is based upon the fact that SAP has been selling licenses at a rate of around 100 a month for the past two years and

implementation projects run from one to three years. By this count, there are roughly two thousand five hundred companies in North America currently implementing SAP in one fashion or another, and a preponderance of these companies are large ones.

Estimating the supply of experienced SAP consultants is not an easy task. Lumping all consultants together is also misleading. There are project managers, integration specialists, Basis gurus, and consultants who specialize in FI, CO, SD, MM, PP, HR, PM, et al. Prior to 1996, there were about a thousand projects and the number of experienced consultants has therefore risen in the neighborhood of six or eight thousand consultants. Add five or six thousand previously experienced consultants and you come with 11,000 to 14,000. Our guess is that the truest number is the lower of these two.

Any North American with more than two years of solid SAP experience (i.e. a mix of configuration skills and business skills) is a rare find. Rarer still are SAP consultants with a) prior industry background and b) real consulting experience.

Where SAP Consultants Come From

The catch-word in all of this is 'experience.' What kind of experience do these consultants bring to the table? Every week, our firm receives resumes that are filled with SAP initials such as FI or SD or MM and we have to analyze the contents of these resumes with magnifying glasses. Ellie, our administrative assistant, patiently answers phone calls from candidates who want highly-paid careers in Sap (rhymes with rap), the first hint that their touted experience is hardly genuine. Other candidates claim to have a year or more of SAP experience but interviews reveal that they were merely in a company that was implementing SAP and had little direct involvement.

There is a simple reason why so many people are presenting themselves as SAP consultants. Look around the work areas where any SAP implementation is taking place and you will see press clippings about the high cost of SAP consulting pinned or taped to walls. Ka-ching. SAP and money are also synonymous.

 On a Manhattan street I was once offered a diamond ring for fifty dollars. I asked the salesman if I could scratch the ring on a nearby marble column. He asked why and I replied that I wanted to see if the diamond was real. Who, he asked indignantly, was talking about 'real?'

SAP is an economic whirlwind, and thus attracts anyone who wants to ride a fast track to power and wealth. As such, there are more sources for SAP consultants than might otherwise be assumed. In fact, the North American SAP market is rife with charlatans, body-shoppers, and just plain slave traders. It is useful to know where consultants truly come from so you can better distinguish the zircons from the diamonds.

1. Converted IS Consultants

Consulting firms did not take long to see the money train that SAP could become and many of them created SAP practices by orienting existing IS staff to SAP.

The immediate assumption is that IS professionals are natural candidates for SAP consulting, but this is not quite true. As we stress elsewhere, success in an SAP implementation requires business knowledge, not technical knowledge. People from the IS world whose strengths are technical rather than business-oriented may not succeed in SAP. File design, programming specifications, and programming are such peripheral issues as to be almost non-existent in the world of SAP.

By contrast, IS professionals whose strengths are strategic planning, functional design, user coordination, and the like tend to find their useful niche in SAP endeavors.

2. SAP Implementation Team Members

A large contingency of SAP consultants in the field today came from the ranks of companies that have implemented SAP. Some of the people were displaced from their old jobs by the project and drifted into consulting. Others, taking note of the salaries of SAP consultants on their projects, leaped from their companies once they were able to put '1 year of SAP experience' on their resumes.

These consultants bring a mixed bag to the table. They have SAP experience in only one environment, their former company. Normally, they would have started the SAP project already having mastered the terrain of their own company. They may not be quite so nimble or effective when they find themselves parachuting into *your* company, where they will not know the business context and therefore will be slow to proceed.

There are three elements of SAP consulting that should be addressed:

- industry background

- SAP knowledge

- consulting skills

Consulting can be a slinky-dinky endeavor, in which the consultant feels obliged to make everyone happy at the cost of project success. People coming straight from industry are consulting neophytes and will often tend to think that 'satisfying the user' is the aim, when in point of fact the aim is to 'serve the client.' Arbitration, presentation, education, clarification, negotiation, compromise, documentation, and resolve are consulting requirements that only experience can provide.

This is not to say that such consultants are to be avoided. On the contrary, they often have their feet more firmly on the ground than life-long consultants. You should merely be cautioned that an SAP experience alone does not make a consultant.

3. Engineers

It is no longer surprising to find that the most successful SAP consultants include a large number of people coming from the field of engineering. 'How things work' is at the core of SAP success, and engineers are, by training and experience, talented at getting to 'how things work.' They will not rely as much on IT as on the flow of work, and this is to their advantage.

If you find an SAP consultant who has industry background, some consulting experience, solid SAP knowledge, and an engineering pedigree, sign him or her on the dotted line and blow on the ink to dry it as fast as possible.

4. Schooled Consultants

This is a category of consultants to avoid, not because they are all bad at what they do, but because it is so difficult to gauge, prior to taking them on, how effective they might be. The Big 6 has a lot of such people, as does any large consulting company where the notion of 'green beans' is applied. It is fine to accept these people on your project at vastly reduced rates. Many will prove useful and worth the cost; others will merely be gaining experience at your expense. If your team has more than one such person for every five seasoned consultants, give your project management that baleful glare that you usually reserve for nasty waiters you intend to stiff.

5. The European Connection

The announcement of R/3 did not create a firestorm in Europe because SAP's R/2 was already widely implemented. In 1993, around 70% of the top 500 companies in Germany had already licensed SAP, for example. Imagine.

The European consulting pool is therefore wider and deeper than the North American pool and great numbers of these consultants have been tabbed for implementations on this side of the water. Their SAP knowledge and experience can be of huge benefit, most particularly as regards the relative depth of that experience.

The flip side is that the consulting skills brought by Europeans do not always match North American needs. Implementation methods vary from country to country because cultures vary and implementations are undertaken by groups and not individuals. One European used to complain to me that Americans are such fantasists and do not face reality squarely. What he was referring to is our penchant for corporate consensus rather than corporate obedience. I advised this consultant to learn patience and to replace the word 'fantasist' with 'free-wheeling.'

A number of Europeans point out that the foundation of SAP is a collection of best business practices, yet North American firms tend to ignore this and go about installing SAP to fit business practices that are unique to them. Stubborn individuality is an American characteristic that extends to companies and the way they are run and it is true that our insistence upon our 'unique' aspects is at odds with SAP principles. The Europeans are looking to conform while we are looking to reform. European consultants who understand this can be highly successful. Those who do not will chafe and probably fail.

In closing:

Pursuing the question of 'experience,' we feel compelled to add that a certain misguided snobbery about SAP experience is widespread. People with as little as one year of SAP background tend to look down upon anyone with less experience than they, as if SAP experience alone elevates a consultant to knighthood. Some of this attitude is the result of SAP's now defunct 'consulting academies,' which consisted of six weeks of SAP training, at the end of which students were 'certified' as SAP consultants. These academies were badly conceived and poorly executed and many of those who became certified were in no way qualified.

Another element of this misguided snobbery is due to SAP itself. Since mid 1995, when SAP became the biggest and most visible subject of the business and IS press, a redefinition of terms was suddenly in order, having to do with who could or could not represent *the truth*. SAPness slipped into a realm of fog and wonder, and we had the impression that only SAP staff had the truth at their disposal. With apologies to the comedy troupe Monty Python, a Scottish father explains rise of his empire to his son:

FATHER: Listen, lad. I built this kingdom up from nothing. When I started here, all there was was swamp. Other kings said I was daft to build a castle on a swamp, but I built it all the same, just to show 'em. [We signed Big 6 as implementation partners]. It sank into the swamp. So, I built a second one. [We added another big consulting firm's resource] That sank into the swamp. So I built a third one. [With new SAP constraints] That burned down, fell over, then sank into the swamp. But the fourth one...[using serious SAP experienced firms] stayed up! And that's what you're gonna get, lad: the strongest castle in these islands.　　　　　Courtesy, *Monty Python and the Holy Grail*

Professional experience, in industry and in consulting, that precedes SAP experience will add weight to that experience. You should cast a baleful eye on any resume that includes less than four years of industry experience preceding SAP experience. There will always be exceptions; talent is never distributed evenly by the gods, nor is professionalism. Stars are often prima donnas; troopers are under-esteemed.

In a general sense, consultants are not what they used to be: seasoned heavyweights with a string of accomplishments who can bring you instant insight and an immediate return on investment. Nowadays, consultants are (at worst) a few months ahead of you or (at best) clear-sighted, responsible folks with an expertise to share with you.

Our most earnest advice is to avoid the extremes at either end: the massive consulting companies that tend to rely on schooled consultants and the charlatan body-shoppers who deal in SAP contracts while clearing $10 to $20 per hour per consultant for themselves. Neither is working in a partnership with you. Both are fleecing you. Beware.

Choosing Your Consulting Partner

The size and location of your company will play some role in determining the options you have in choosing consultants. If you are in a multi-billion dollar enterprise and the bulk of your project will take place in a major city, you will have access to the larger consulting firms

as well as the middle-sized and small firms that specialize in SAP. All the same, you cannot expect that any one of these companies will have all the consultants you need when you need them. The supply of qualified consultants does not begin to meet the demand. Further, SAP consultants are not generalists. If you are implementing FI, SD, MM, PP, and HR, you will probably be looking for expertise in each of these areas.

Therefore, your first rule when choosing a consulting partner, is to take a close look at the proposed consultants and not just the firm that presents them. You should be interviewing each consultant to determine whether not the candidate is the right fit. It helps considerably if the people doing the interviewing have some knowledge of SAP. One suggestion is that you engage another consulting group to help you with the selection. This other group would of course have to be eliminated from any consideration as the implementation partner in order to be sure that its recommendations are objective.

Interviewing the candidates will also help you to avoid the bait-and-switch method sometimes used during proposals, in which prime consultants present their firm and show off their SAP dance steps but are not among those who show up at your door to dance with you after Day One.

You will also have to be realistic. In the spring of 1996, we received a number of requests for help in the area of Human Resource. Nearly all of these requests included the proviso that the consultants had to have at least a year of experience in the 3.0 release. No one could be found for the simple reason that release 3.0 had only been around for five or six months. Nevertheless, the clients continued to insist on a full year of 3.0 experience.

Most consulting firms will peddle a combination of project management, consultants, and methodologies. Look carefully at this last item because the cost of your project can rise significantly based upon its contents. More on this later.

Your Audit Partner and the SAP Pie

All North American firms of any appreciable size will have an audit firm and a great number of these firms have consulting practices. Given the money associated with SAP, many of them have consultants to offer you. These firms have an inside track because they have prior knowledge of your practices and your people. They also have that big audit stick to hold over your head.

It is tempting to simply engage this group as your SAP implementation partner on the premise that you can avoid having multiple consulting companies flitting around your offices. This would make sense if it were not for the fact that no consulting firm will have all the consultants you need when you need them. Further, consultants from your audit firm have easier access to your executives than do consultants from elsewhere. They can influence your decisions regarding the project and your consultants even if they haven't been engaged to do so.

It makes better sense to assess consulting firms on their merits. Can they offer qualified, experienced implementers? Is the team they are offering configured to your needs or according to standard practice? Can they provide a project approach that fits your business context, or do they use a cookie-cutter method that could apply to any client?

Whatever your intentions, you will most certainly feel the heat of your audit partner throughout the duration of the project, most particularly if your implementation is entrusted to a consulting firm that has its own audit practice as well.

In either case, keep a close eye on consulting *partner* fees. These usually range between $3,000 and $5,000 per day. What you get in return is often of dubious value, such as the time that partners spend grilling their consultants about additional consulting potential on your site or the time partners spend with you gassing about 'project progress'. If more than one 'partner' day per fifty days of other consultants is included in the proposal, look more closely at the rest of the proposal with an eye out for fat.

Your Project Manager: Decision # 1

The single most important decision you will make in an SAP implementation project is this: who will be your project manager?

It is the project manager who:

- is the prime architect of the project plan
- allocates and directs resources to fulfill that project plan
- orchestrates the rhythm and tone of project progress and team cohesion
- manages the scope of effort
- manages the expectations of users and management
- determines the source and disposition of resources, both internal and external.

The project manager must be the daily guardian of the vision that you wish to fulfill. As such, you need to be fairly certain that this manager will remain with you to the end of the project. Further, there should be an element of trust between the project manager and upper management, most especially since the project manager will probably be supplied from the outside, i.e. an SAP consulting firm. Without trust, upper management will tend to wonder if the project manager is acting in the client's interest or in the interest of the consulting firm.

While you are going through the selection process, be aware that project management is the battleground for rival consulting firms. The firm that provides project management will be the one that later takes credit for the 'successful implementation'. More to the point, this firm will have a major influence on the source and disposition of consultants.

Even after your choice of a project manager has been made, he or she will be the target of criticism from within and without. Some criticism is normal because of the natural resistance to the change that the project will include. More of the criticism will be derived from a desire on the part of other firms to place their own project manager. If you are in upper management and are in a position to decide about who or who does not manage your project, you should measure the motives of whoever is attacking your project manager and act accordingly.

It is also advisable to provide your project manager with an internal sidekick, one of your own people who will eventually inherit the warclub while the initial project manager slips back into an advisory role or disappears altogether.

The fortunes of most implementation projects tend to rise or fall according to the quality of project management as well as the level of trust between upper management and the project manager.

Multi-Partner Consulting Teams

As previously mentioned, few SAP implementations take place with a single consulting firm helping out. The high demand and low supply of consultants almost guarantees that a client will need to form a team derived from two or more firms and then find a way to turn them into a single, focused unit.

Consultants from diverse firms may have difficulties working with those from another. Differences range from the technical to the tribal and you will have to address them, and eliminate them, as quickly as

possible or your project will slip off track. Some clients apportion different sub-projects to different consulting firms and thus avoid friction between the teams by keeping them separate. This will not work seamlessly because of the integration factor. If one consulting team is configuring FI and another SD and another still MM, final integration of these applications will be difficult.

It is preferable to mix the consultants into an effective single team, establish a single project approach to be adhered to by all concerned, and firmly impress upon one and all that the project belongs to the client and not to whatever firm the consultant is representing.

Consultants who fail to respect your guidelines and who insist too much upon their firm's methods and practices should be removed from the project. Consultants with strong team skills and lesser SAP skills are preferable to those with strong SAP skill and lesser teaming skills.

Seven Cautions

The level of assistance you receive from consultants is up to you and not them. You can configure your project team with a mix of qualified consultants placed in their proper slots, or you can throw an army of consultants at the problem and hope for the best. The companies that cite consultants as the cause of implementation failure should look homeward. Following are some things to watch for when configuring your team.

Caution #1

CONSULTANTS MAY NOT BE AS EXPERIENCED AS ADVERTISED AND ARE THUS RECEIVING ON-THE-JOB TRAINING AT THE EXPENSE OF THE CLIENT.

This is a particularly common occurrence for SAP jobs in North America for two reasons; first, because SAP is a relatively new system here and experienced SAP consultants are hard to find; second, the high demand for bonafide experience in SAP has pushed the costs ever higher. Greed has appeared in too many quarters and truly inexperienced consultants are being pushed into projects and into situations in which they cannot succeed.

What to Do:

Interview all prospective consultants before allowing them to join your project. If you know little of SAP, hire consultants to assist you in the interview process. Do not 'leave it to the experts.'

Caution # 2

MANAGEMENT CONSULTANTS MAY PROPOSE ADD-ON ACTIVITIES OR SUB-PROJECTS WHICH SEEM ATTRACTIVE AT THE OUTSET BUT MAY BE OF DUBIOUS VALUE TO THE DEFINED PROJECT.

In this same regard, project over runs are, sadly, in the best interests of some consulting firms. The longer the project, the higher the billing. Whether intentional or not, consultants may widen or change the scope of the project, particularly in the course of long term projects, during which the client situation is continuing to evolve.

What to Do:

Assess new proposals within the context of the project, not as isolated to their own merits. You can build almost anything with the SAP erector set and add-on proposals in the course of a project tend to address expanded functionality. Accept those that make economic sense and reject those that have the feel of 'wouldn't it be nice'.

If new proposals address the solution to project problems such as user or management resistance, education, or communication, give them your full attention. These are 'fester' subjects that may require the allocation of time and resources, to the detriment of the project plan and budget, but to the benefit of the overall success of the project.

Caution # 3

LARGE CONSULTING FIRMS NORMALLY HAVE THEIR OWN IN-HOUSE METHODOLOGIES, ESPECIALLY FOR SYSTEMS PROJECTS. At times, the client is charged for use of these methodologies. This is reasonable only if the methodology applies to the defined project. To our knowledge, the only existing methodology for SAP implementation is the SAP Implementation Guide, which in itself is incomplete (as it says, a *guide* not a methodology). Other methodologies are for classical design, development, and implementation projects and would not be efficient for use in an SAP implementation.

What to Do:

If the methodology is comprised of forms and scripts in fat, multi-volume binders, give it a long, hard look. Assess the consulting firm's approach to the project. How much transfer of SAP knowledge is called for? At what point and to what depth is a gap analysis called for? Is the AS-IS phase viewed as lengthy?

If the methodology addresses the creation of 'deliverables' (i.e. documents), it is probably a revised version of a classical methodology and should be rejected.

It would also be helpful to get a second opinion from another consulting firm. As with the interviewing process, this would necessarily be a firm that will offer an objective view and has nothing to gain by trashing the proposed methodology .

What you want to avoid is a project that tends to fulfill the steps described by a methodology but fails to fulfill your project aims. Even an acceptable methodology will call for activities and tasks that are not needed for a given project. Reconfigure the methodology according to your scope throughout the project, not only at the beginning.

Caution #4

WHEN MORE THAN ONE CONSULTING GROUP IS RETAINED, CLASHES AS TO PROJECT METHODS AND TOOLS MAY ARISE.

Project tasks devoted to proving the advisability of one method over another add little value to the defined project.

What to Do:

When multiple partners are engaged, one or another must be assigned the role of lead partner and single project approach should be established. If secondary partners do not adhere to the chosen project approach, purge them. Multiple partners should not be leading you in multiple directions.

Caution # 5

CLIENTS CAN BECOME DEPENDENT UPON OUTSIDE CONSULTANTS, BEYOND THE SCOPE OF THE PROJECT, if SAP knowledge isn't transferred from consulting staff to client staff.

Very efficient consultants may tend to accomplish the work themselves, for the sake of time and efficiency. Without an adequate transfer of SAP knowledge, the presence of outside consultants may be extended well beyond the completion of the defined project.

What to Do:

As mentioned throughout this book, you should plan on transfer of knowledge from the beginning. If your staff has had sufficient training to SAP and been able to get a grip on the consultant share of the project, you will be fine. If serious SAP training has not taken place, your consultant dependency will be a dicey affair, difficult to gauge, and more difficult to end.

Make certain that your people are doing the real configuration, *guided* by consultants. The sole exception to this scenario is the off-site configuration that is often done for middle-sized companies, in which, all the same, your staff will need to know what has been done prior to final implementation.

Caution #6

PROJECT DEADLINES CAN SLIP AND CLIENTS TEND TO WONDER IF THESE SLIPPAGES ARE CAUSED BY CONSULTANT STAFF OR THEIR OWN STAFF. In some cases these slippages are due to optimistic allocations of client staff in the master plan, in other cases because of consultant mistakes or oversights. Consultants tend to presume the former.

What to Do:

Assume the worst and plan on slippages. When they occur, measure whether or not the client staff has indeed fulfilled its charge. If not, give the consultants a break, regroup, and push ahead.

Caution #7

AT THE OUTSET OF A LONG TERM PROJECT, THE PROJECT PLAN IS BASED UPON ANTICIPATION AND PAST EXPERIENCE. Through the long duration, many tasks that were planned become pointless and yet are carried out because they were included in the plan. Consultants may see the completion of these tasks as a contractual obligation.

What to Do:

Cancel the tasks, inform the consultants that you are doing so and why, and re-direct resources.

What Consultants Should Do For You

Consultants provide experience with SAP to shorten the user and IS learning curve and accelerate the project delivery. Their experience with projects of this breadth and complexity reduces the risk of the project. Consultants provide project methodology, project tracking, techniques for executing the project and they understand the methodology and tools that are inherent to SAP.

Consultants should best be used to facilitate not only the implementation but the company's transformation to an SAP environment by accomplishing a **knowledge transfer**. For such a transfer to successfully take place, a rough equivalence of one consultant to one to three in-house persons should be envisioned, bearing in mind that the consultant will disappear once the transfer of knowledge has occurred.

If, at some point just before Day One use of SAP, your company's staff is self-reliant in terms of the uses and techniques of SAP configuring and business modeling, then you might conclude that judicious use of consultants has taken place. If, however, your company is still reliant on consultants, then either the consultants have failed, or are clinging to their positions on the project, or you have not sufficiently achieved the transfer of knowledge. The fault can also be that in-house staff is just not picking up the reins; again, leaving it to the experts.

You Want to Know About Consulting Rates

Your basic and capable SAP implementation consultant is going to cost you in the neighborhood of:

- per hour rate
- two flights a week
- four nights of hotel
- eight to ten meals, depending upon breakfast habits
- maybe a rental car, maybe some extras

Deal with it.

Your higher level consultants will cost you all the same as above, but bump you $25 an hour for primo consultants, or $50 more (and more) for management level. Deal with that as well. Interview these people up front (see other chapters that deal with this), but when you find what you need, pay it. The final cost is not in these consultants, it is in your project direction and how you make use of these consultants that will make it worth the cost or not. We talk with our partnered consultants on a regular basis and find too often that their talents are being wasted by poor project management, and so do what we can to redirect them to proper projects, i.e. projects that have direction.

Please follow the life of an SAP implementation consultant:

Monday AM: early early early rising, like 4 to 5 AM to catch a flight to wherever the hell you are going.

Monday mid-day: arrival at your work site, catch up on the first three hours of your day.

Monday evening: still catching up, and very probably tearing out hair and trying to make sense of what they missed while they were on the plane.

Monday night: a hotel room. HBO. Odd food. Orange shag carpeting.

Tuesday AM: showered and ready. Hits the ground, and stays there, hard and fast through...

....Friday AM, having spent ten to twelve hours per day since Tuesday AM banging away at your situation. Same bad orange shag carpeting in the hotel room and sometimes worse, like the breakfast was not ready or the hotel failed to give them the wake up call. Knot the tie and comb the hair and/or apply the blush, slip on the loafers or heels or tennis shoes, and head off to your company. All the while, your project suffers from internal and possibly poor management, and almost certainly a serious lack of SAP knowledge and background. So, your consultant is doing his or her best to put the discourse into business terms, because the consultant is not there to simply pass the time and your project better be up to snuff because these good people have better things to do than piss away their careers on badly managed projects. If so, they will...

...fly out each Friday at noon or thereabouts, thinking, the hell with you. And rightly so.

In the interim, note, the consultant is *away from home* for a full week to do service to your firm. While you are looking at rates, this consultant is looking at you, hard, from Monday evening at the latest and through the remaining hotel-filled week.

Do not, repeat, do not treat oncoming consultants as suspect mercenaries. Embrace them, integrate them, show them where the coffee room is to be found, take the time to initiate them to whatever stage of the project that they find themselves thrust into, give them a week or so to get a feel for the tasks they are expected to fulfill, add another whole day to explain to them the objectives of the overall project, and you will give them a horizon toward which they can work. You do not have the upper hand just because you hold the paycheck. You are simply the client, not the master.

This seems like dim-witted, simple, advice. It is not. We have often seen the situation, in which consultants are interviewed, screened, accepted, ticketed, and shipped off to client sites. At those client sites the consultants are given poor assignments with little measureable criteria for success—all at high hourly rates. This situation is not good for the client or the consultant.

You are going to pay these consultant rates far too long and for far too much if you do not direct them into the proper work paths. You are going to pay these consultants rates far too long and for far too much if you do not invest in the education of your own staff so that you can say adios to the consultants within a proper time-frame.

Enough about rates. What are you going to do with the resources you buy? The onus of consultants, how they are employed and how they are utilized, is on you, mate, not the consultants.

Distinguishing North from South

*How to Avoid Walking in the Usual Circles
Until You Drop*

The Pitfalls of the GAP Analysis

In our previous 'tome,' *In the Path of the Whirlwind, an Apprentice Guide to the World of SAP*, we made several serious points about the usual obsession with a twenty percent shortfall between "required" software and "available" software.

"..it is presumed that no package will fit more than 80% of a company's needs, and so the remaining elusive, unique-to-you, 20% has to be designed and developed separately.

Too often, companies have failed to forge ahead with new software acquisition because of an obsession over that 20%. Instead of looking at the broader picture of how a new and dynamic 80% solution will improve company performance, they have waited, or searched for a package that just might do it all."

121

The bottom line is that companies draw up their requirements and then go searching for software that will satisfy those requirements. They never find a 100% solution. They generally find an 80% solution.

This is where the GAP analysis comes into play. It is the object of that missing 20% of functionality. In a classical systems approach, you would be tempted to create a specification to fill the gap between your chosen software and the missing functionality, to develop software to fill that gap, and insert it into your final total systems solution, as if 80 + 20 = 100.

The difficulty is that by the time you have:

- identified the gaps
- designed patches to fill the gaps
- programmed patches to fill the gaps
- implemented the other 80% and
- implemented the patched 20%…

…but in that same time period your company, and the business environment in which it works, will have changed. And the 20% will have shifted into something new, another set of gaps altogether.

The pursuit of this elusive 20% is perpetual. It is the daily challenge of those who deal in information systems.

It is difficult to make a proper GAP analysis, and harder still to come up with a tenable design to fill that gap. Even if the final system meets your needs one hundred percent, you know quite well that your satisfaction will not be long-lasting. If it were possible to achieve 100%

satisfactory systems, even for a minute, time would have to be standing still.

When it comes to SAP, this situation is exacerbated to the nth degree. SAP is vast, and its vastness alone defies the creation and maintenance of a true GAP analysis. All the same, too many project managers launch just such an analysis at a point in the project in which *they still do not know jack about SAP.*

For a long and uncomfortable stretch, we had a half dozen of our better consultants partnered into a major implementation project. Five or six of the bigger firms were more firmly entrenched at the client site and two of them constantly sent their consultants to meet with ours to ask whether or not SAP could or could not fulfill a given business requirement. Our consultants answered questions as best they could and then their interviewers hustled off to tell the client that SAP could not fulfill their needs, so new entries were added to the 'gap analysis'.

In essence, neither the client nor the frontline consultants had sufficient SAP background to make the call. But the implementation partner's methodology insisted upon a GAP analysis at this point in the project. This began in the fourth month of a three-year project, and the client was still more than moist behind the ears. All the same, a voluminous GAP analysis was issued and untold gazillions were committed to sub-projects intended to fill those gaps the way wood glue might fill the holes caused by termites.

As the project progressed, the front line consulting firms were replaced by other consultants (including our own) with real SAP experience. It was discovered that the majority of previously-identified 'gaps' were illusory and the sub-projects launched to fill them were a waste of time and money.

The problem was that the client and its initial front line consultants were suffering from a *knowledge gap*.

There *will* be gaps that SAP alone cannot bridge. As a configurable software (and there is still only one version of it) it cannot serve every client completely. Take a look at the materials master file, for example, and your concerns may evolve into full-blown panic. As you begin to configure the system, you will find that key pieces in the erector set just plain aren't there. Whether you choose to replace these pieces with bolt-ons, ABAP patches, or the purchase of additional software (which will of course require interfacing), will depend upon just how wide the gap is.

The caution here is that you cannot identify many of these gaps in the early months of your implementation project. You most certainly cannot identify them prior to acquiring the software unless you make a serious upfront investment in SAP education so that your knowledge gap has already been narrowed.

Strong consulting help will save you time and money in this regard. Experienced consultants will identify *true* gaps between what you need and what SAP can deliver. Less experienced consultants may scratch their heads and suggest ABAP programming (and the consequent maintenance headaches).

Another caution: if you are asking SAP representatives of the sales persuasion whether or not the impending upgrade of SAP will fill a currently-perceived gap, the response will probably be positive. This may very well be true because the functionality of SAP is widened and honed at a rapid pace. Provide SAP with a query in writing and ask for a response in writing before you count on an upgrade that will fill your functional gap.

Three Hundred Alices, or The Negotiation Gap

You are an SD module leader and your mission is to present SAP to Alice, the head of sales order processing. Alice has been with the company for a number of years and has worked on three different information systems. She knows her business and she knows her system and she is not particularly pleased with what she's heard about the SAP implementation project.

Further, someone's told you that Alice doesn't like you very much.

She comes to your office and you offer her coffee but she prefers tea. You lean to your notes and she looks at her watch. You can't help but notice she is wearing a pin with the company logo on her lapel. These pins are given out by the CEO as awards for long and meritorious service to the company. As you power up your desktop, Alice asks if this is really going to take all morning. With a nervous smile, you begin to demo the current prototype for sales order entry and verification. On another screen, Alice lights up her current system. As you describe your new process for order entry, Alice compares her current system to your prototype. She is making points faster than a digital pinball machine with a lit bonus. Your SAP system requires her to pass through two screens and a query compared to her current system in which everything happens on a single screen. On her current system, the order date is in the upper left hand corner of the screen. On your prototype, it is sitting dead center. Her current system includes a forty character 'Notes' field that she considers the key to her success. Your prototype has no field for notes and, shaken, you forget to point out the documentation subsystem that is built into just about every facet of the software.

For the next few hours, you hem and haw with her about various functions. Finally, she challenges you to a race. She will enter five new orders in the time it takes you to enter three.

What do you do with Alice? Do you return to the project conference room and hit the drawing board with an ABAP patch? Has Alice truly pointed out a series of gaps that have be addressed?

No way. What Alice has done is demonstrate her mastery of the present tense, a tense that is vertical, isolated, and destined to disappear. She is defending sales order entry; you are representing workflow.

We tell this story in our seminars and, very recently, one of the attendees burst forth with the rejoinder, "We've got three hundred Alices in our company." Our advice to all of you with one or a thousand Alices is: teach them the joys of workflow. With a certain panache, insist upon what you believe. You are following a vision; Alice is repeating past experience.

Do not become fixated on a comparison of minor processes. Talk to Alice about her communication and reporting requirements. You will find that she:

- makes a weekly report to the finance folks as to order portfolio

- gets a dozen calls a day from the credit department asking for info on various clients

- prepares a monthly report on sales order activity by region, by product group, and by sales rep on spreadsheet that she wrote and maintains herself

- modifies more than half of her sales orders because her systems do not provide sufficient product data to allow for confirmed orders on the first go

- calls the clients on a regular basis to be sure they have received their order acknowledgements and that planned delivery dates are acceptable.

Your prototype should address these issues and these issues should be the subject between you and Alice, not the simple process of how an order is entered into the system. You will very possibly have found that electronic data interchange (EDI) will eliminate a significant portion of the entry anyhow.

What you must not do is note down all of Alice's objections and scroll them into a modification spec. Alice needs programming in most cases, not SAP. She needs to know that once SAP is implemented, she will be concentrating on exceptions rather than the basic flow of simple and obvious orders, that SAP itself, in its integrated way, will provide data to those who, at present, dial her number to pick her brains. Alice has to learn where she sits in the cycles of your company's workflow. And she has to accept some of the take in order to benefit from the give.

It is true that there are thousands of routines that SAP will satisfy in an unsatisfactory fashion. Ergonomics for minor processes often go by the wayside. This is the flip side of tightly integrated software. It is also the stumbling point of consultants and other implementers on a daily basis. We have heard several variations of the phrase, "SAP is ugly sometimes, but it works."

The difficulty is that Alice becomes the roadblock, not the process. And, let's face it, Alices come in all flavors. Some quite simply need to be educated to the wonders of workflow and you will have a major ally in your corner. Others, bewildered and angry by the change in the labor scenery, will bludgeon you with these minor process comparisons and stall your project indefinitely. If you cave in and start fiddling overmuch with SAP, you will very possibly mollify Alice while adding needless cost to your project and the longer term maintenance of your system.

Shifting from a vertical to a horizontal point of view takes time for everyone. When it comes to implementations like these, the customer may be right in the present tense, but dead wrong in the future tense. Make diplomatic concessions where feasible. Address ergonomic points where possible. But firmly hold the line on workflow points.

AS IS—or "The Way We Were"

Vast numbers of SAP implementations include this pair of phases: AS IS and TO BE. There is an on-going discussion in our company about the usefulness of an AS IS phase for a SAP implementation.

For the uninitiated, an AS IS phase (formerly referred to in a wordier fashion as a 'Current State Analysis') is a phase in which all or part of the client business processes are analyzed, charted, and scripted. In essence, it is a complete inventory of the current way a company functions.

There *are* reasons for an AS IS phase if it is intelligently applied:

- major processes should be charted *and quantified* in order to measure potential benefits of new processes which will be enabled by SAP;

- unless your consultants are greatly skilled in your company's industry, AS IS allows the consultants and your internal project team—often for their first time—to truly understand your company's major business processes;

- detailed scripting is not really necessary; a broad understanding of the business processes presented in a wall flow chart is the goal;

- AS IS often helps set the boundaries and expectations for the TO BE phase;

- if your staff is involved in subsequent BPR, some experience in charting and scripting business processes will be useful; using your existing business processes as a source will allow them some known territory for a first experience at BPR.

Avoid Paying Through the Nose for AS IS

Traditionally, the TO BE phase follows the AS IS phase. TO BE requires you and your consultants to take the vision of the company and chart and script how it will work once SAP is configured. As the theory goes, you will use the AS IS documents as a basis for the TO BE.

129

Most project plans include the following steps:

One Stair Too Many

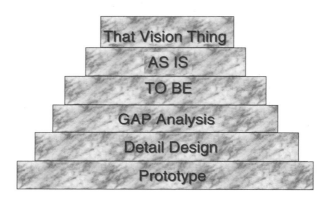

From a vision to a prototype application of that vision, you are descending from the abstract to the concrete in a fairly direct fashion. You have your eyes not only on the road ahead but on the far horizon of the future. All except for the AS IS, which is a rear-view mirror. After coming up with a vision for what your company will become, you should be heading toward the vision with firm steps. But when the next is AS IS, you can quickly become side-tracked.

If AS IS goes on too long and you are not merely charting the current business processess for broad understanding, your AS IS phase has become overblown. AS IS has become what we call "The Consulting Partner's Retirement Fund Phase because it is proceeding at great cost in time, money and energy and will yield little in benefit.

What happens during an overblown AS IS phase? First, you make a full inventory of what you are all about, how you work, what you do, how much time and money it takes for each step and process. Then you lay it all out, point a finger at the weaknesses, scratch a few arrows from one step to another, and figure out how you are going to make it better. You are scratching and clawing from the AS IS to the TO BE, from the now to the then, from the known present to the glittering future.

The bottom line of the overblown AS IS: you have paid consultants to ask your people questions about how you work, and to make charts and scripts of the same and immediately thereafter you will throw those charts and scripts into dead-letter files, because with SAP you will no longer work that way. It serves you little and costs you a small fortune. And the minute you turn the project page, your AS IS becomes an AS WAS—'The Way we Were.'

It's too painful to reme hem ber
the huh way we weeeeeerrre

So watch out for the downside of an overblown AS IS:

- It is probably more difficult to chart an 'overblown' AS IS than it is to chart a viable TO BE. So why waste the time and money to inventory what you are intent upon dumping? Proper use of SAP tends to show that tradition tends to disappear.

- You may think your company is complicated and unique. Most people feel that way about their companies. An overblown AS IS may make the company appear unnecessarily complicated and provide the traditionalists with data to attempt to keep things the same. Proper use of SAP tends to make some traditions fade away.

- An overblown AS IS will tend to be filled with incremental improvements rather than radical improvements. There is nothing creative to an AS IS and if it is used as a basis for the TO BE, you may not look upon your business activity with a fresh point of view. Traditions will remain in place and you will find yourselves tinkering instead of creating.

As we discussed earlier, a proper GAP analysis requires upfront knowledge of SAP. A useful AS IS phase requires restraint. If you are in the midst of choosing an implementation partner from among a group of consulting firms, take a look at how they position these phases in their proposals. If the GAP analysis is to occur too early in the project or a detailed AS IS has been suggested by the consultants, just remember this:

While choosing your consulting partner, you are the fisherman. By ignoring this advice, you may later be only bait for a useless Gap analysis and a costly AS IS.

Only You Can Prevent Forest Fires

How Scope Ignites During SAP Implementations

If You See Ice Cream, You Want Ice Cream

A recent survey revealed that a vast number of Americans eat dinner only so that they can have their dessert. Everything that precedes dessert is simply groundwork and dues-paying. Dinner is the means and dessert the end.

I am not a part of that statistic. I am usually intent on the appetizer, the main course, and perhaps the wine. I never think of dessert unless I find myself in a restaurant in England, where they tend to pull a dessert trolley close to the table once the main course is half finished. There I sit, picking over the last of my boiled meat and potatoes (English cuisine *is* an oxymoron) and my eye falls upon a mad swirl of mousse au chocolat, drifts to a creme anglaise, meanders to an apple tart. The meat that I was so contentedly chewing turns suddenly gray in my mouth. I look away but my eyes inevitably drift back. Say, miss, is that a chocolate cake? Ah, choco-mint! I set down my fork and sigh. With vanilla ice cream, please.

I may see the names of each of these desserts on a menu beforehand, but the words alone do not inspire my want of them. Only when they are laid out before me, and for a long enough time to tempt me, do I tend to *need* them.

So it is, during an SAP implementation, when functions or features that you never particularly wanted turn to needs before you know it. If you are not careful and focused, the vision of where you are heading will become clouded with a variety of tempting desserts.

The phrase 'scope creep' is fairly common and is applied by most people to mean: a sneaky, insidious widening of scope, barely detectable on a day-to-day basis, usually caused by user needs that are not anticipated or could not be avoided if the project is to succeed.

When you see functionality, you want functionality, whether you need it or not. The vast depth and breadth of SAP functionality is breathtaking, and endlessly tempting. Changes in scope do not creep in during an SAP implementation, they explode in your face.

Ways in Which Scope Ignites During an SAP Implementation

1. You need a camp fire and gather kindling.

SAP invites radical improvement of business processes, yet most companies start out looking for incremental improvement. The initial project scope is consequently limited and lacking in ambition and can only expand.

2.   You figure out that if you throw more sticks into the fire it will burn higher and hotter.

As the project progresses and the SAP learning curve kicks in, clients discover the full potential at their fingertips and want more.

3. The scouts you have hired point out nifty ways to play with the fire.

The company is distracted from its initial vision by consultants seeking to change or expand or refine that vision. This can be useful or detrimental.

4. The chiefs of the tribe want to make sure there's enough fire for them, so they light their own camp fires.

As new business process design is understood by upper management, the notion that SAP functionality equals power leads to new sub-projects.

5. One group enthusiastically creates a bonfire that is noticed by other groups, who begin creating their own bonfires.

The learning curve is mastered by your project staff and the SAP functionality forest is plundered.

6. One campfire blazes out of control and all hands have to leave their campfires to extinguish it.

One aspect of the project has become unmanageable and stalls the over-all project progression.

7. The chiefs banish a portion of the tribe and there aren't enough fire tenders to go around.

Pre-mature downsizing leads to a shortage of manpower to handle the expanded scope of the project.

8. The village burns to the ground.

Scope Management

The expansion of project scope is inevitable and you can manage that expansion to the benefit of your company only if you are prepared for it.

 First of all, someone has to be given the authority to manage scope. This can be one person but would best be a group of people with enough involvement in the project to understand the business and SAP issues and a high enough position in the company to comprehend the high level vision.

As the project progresses and the SAP learning curve is on the rise, proposed changes in scope should be referred to the committee, evaluated in terms of cost and benefit, and measured against the current vision in terms of priority. Scope changes that are accepted have to be defined and communicated as do consequent revisions of the project plan and budget.

Here again, if the project commences before your staff and management have been given significant SAP training, the scope will be very difficult to manage because the vast and varied possibilities of what you can do with SAP will reveal themselves on a daily basis. Revelations lead to temptation; temptation leads to revision, and therefore changes in scope.

The difficult aspect of managing scope lies in the fact that not all scope expansions are communicated upward. During the configuring phase, business process designs may not be followed to the letter. This may be due to the fact that SAP cannot do everything under sun in the way you wish it to or because your staff has found functionality that the BPR did not anticipate and that new functionality is embraced *just because it is there for the taking.*

It is important to remember that this functionality will always be there and does not have to be put into play immediately. This is only an implementation project and once it is completed and you are using SAP, the scope of usage can and will expand.

Decide what you need now to support your new business processes. Your needs will change through the long course of the implementation, but somewhere along the line you will have to manage out the brushfires of desire (without totally stamping them out) and follow a determined path to its end.

At the end of that path, you are using SAP, and probably continuing to add or change functionality according to opportunity and circumstances.

In essence, implementation of SAP never ceases. As your business evolves, so will your application of SAP to support it.

The Elements of Scope in an SAP Implementation

Scope is not limited to the number of applications to be implemented and the number of end users who will need to be trained. The following is a short list of factors that will impact your scope throughout an SAP implementation.

1. Sites: Multi-site implementations are obviously lengthier than single site implementations. This is especially so when new business processes cut across multiple sites. If you look at two projects which are identical in every way except that one is single site and the other multi-site, the latter will cost 25% more and take longer to succeed.

2. Number of users: This scope element comes in two waves. First, redesigning business processes for 10 users is vastly simpler than for 1000. Second, and a more pressing item is end user training. However, the mere number of users is less of a factor in scope than might be imagined because, for the most part, users do not come into play until the latter stages of the project. Thus, a company with 1000 users does not have ten times the scope of a company with 100 users except in terms of end user training.

3. Processes: A trading company, which only buys and sells products without having to manufacture and stock them, will consequently have far fewer processes to establish than will a full-fledged manufacturing and distribution enterprise. By the same token, there are varying degrees of manufacturing complexities. Process industries such as oil and gas will pose more headaches than will industries that primarily are concerned with assembly.

4. Applications: FI, CO, MM, and SD are viewed as the core applications that tend to be implemented in every project. Second level applications include PP, MM, and, with the 1996 maturation of 3.0, HR. Third level applications are numerous. Some firms implement in linear fashion, FI, then SD, then MM... Others implement in groups such as FI-SD-MM, then PP and PM or whatever. The order and combination in which you intend to implement will clearly have a major impact on the scope of your project.

5. Expansions and acquisitions: The most difficult variables of scope are these, because the planning of either must be done without the grounding of prior knowledge and experience. Many firms choose SAP as the common-ground solution for a growth-by-acquisition strategy. The starting-point culture of a company to be acquired should be taken into account, as well as the catching-up curve for this company.

6. Reorganizations during the SAP project: You would hope that your company will freeze such activity until business process reengineering can be completed, but it will not happen. There is no way to plan for this, no way to adjust scope until it happens. It *will* happen. Hold your breath.

7. Implementation method (big bang or rollout): Big bangs are scary, but tend to succeed more than rollouts, which are gradual, delaying, and just as high risk as big bangs. The scope question is centered on the users and their readiness to flip the SAP switch. If they are clinging mightily to legacy systems, your scope is widened by the inclusion of security blanket resistance.

Waiter, My Milk is Too Cold

Anyone who has ever waited tables in a restaurant knows that customer expectations span from the standard to the outrageous and often extend into the ludicrous. During my college years, I worked as a waiter in an upscale country club in San Diego. During my second week, one customer of mine ordered a French dip and loudly complained that I had not given him a spoon for his 'soup.' A few days later, another customer protested that his milk was too cold.

Business situations can be just as absurd. I managed my restaurant clients by giving them what they asked: a spoon and warmer milk. This cost my business, the restaurant, nothing more than a few huffy moments of my time. But if, in the course of an SAP implementation, we indulge executives with outrageous or off-the-mark demands, it will cost the company much, much more.

Managing expectations at all levels of the enterprise is one of the most important tasks facing a project manager. Managing *executive* expectations is the most difficult. Executives tend to assume that it is 'an information system' or 'software' or 'something technical that will give us better reports.'

Executive ignorance of what SAP is all about is rampant in North America. Too few SAP buyers take the time to do more than kick the tires before throwing the company behind the wheel. The disappointment curve is established the moment an SAP license is signed and the project is handed off to an implementation team. The gap between this moment and the first crisis meeting is usually three or four months.

The impediments to managing executive expectations are:

• executives do not know what they do not know about SAP;

• they will not take the time to learn more because they do not see the wide scale ramifications of an SAP undertaking (again, thinking of it as IS and not business);

- they assume that the mammoth consulting fees will assure implementation success;

- they assume that cost and time overruns are the responsibility of the implementation team;

- they refuse to see that technology and information are at the core of business, not at the periphery.

Our firm offers seminars on SAP for executives and managers. We are regularly asked if we can provide a one-day seminar—rather that our standard two day—on the premise that these executives do not have the time for *a whole two days*. We note that these same executives are about to engage anywhere from $20 to $200 million for an SAP implementation but only have one day available to collectively educate themselves. This attitude usually extends into the project cycle and is the number one cause of what an hysterical press refers to as 'SAP implementation failures.'

If executives are not brought firmly into the mainstream of the implementation, your scope will expand according to the rise of their curve of disappointment. You will be reordering the workflow of your company and they will be carping about the design of management reports. You will be reducing delivery turnaround by thirty days and they will wonder why you have to spend so much on end user training.

The only way to shorten that curve is to educate them to the reality of the undertaking. If they refuse, you will have to ride the waves of their ignorance throughout the project and accept that, once you have succeeded, these executives will see only the cost and the time spent and will deem your efforts a failure.

The man whose milk was too cold was a petty annoyance in the workflow of a meal being served. A far greater problem is someone

141

who orders what is not even on the menu and refuses to take no for an answer.

Endscope

If you begin with an acceptance that scope will change throughout your project, you will be in a position to manage it. The expansion of functionality is the most natural expansion, and other changes in scope dimension will occur as a direct result of the change in business circumstance throughout the duration of the project.

The project team has to be light on its feet in this regard up through the completion of the configuration phase. Thereafter, we advise that scope be frozen where possible and an 'endscope' be defined and communicated throughout the enterprise. This endscope will disappoint a number of people whose immediate expectations will not be addressed. You will have to address this disappointment with tangible reasons behind the exclusion of whatever elements are viewed as missing. These elements may be addressed at a later time, once critical implementation mass has been completed.

What you should avoid, hereafter, is the continuing loop of expectation to business process re-design to configuration to new expectation. Let the paint dry on the prototype, demonstrate and walk through the prototype with anyone who will listen and learn, and carry on to the end. And then keep going.

:
:
:
:
:
:
:
:

———————

The Brave New World

Cultural and Business Changes That Will Test the Patience of All Concerned

Information, Not Reports

In the early 80s, I was the IS manager for the European trading division of a large British electronics and defense firm, responsible for the information systems for seven different sites from Stockholm to Madrid. In conformance with those times, IS was viewed as subordinate to finance; as such, my main contact at each of the sites was the finance director.

We had developed a single base system for all sites and I found that one of my greatest difficulties in implementation was to get the finance directors to agree on system output, i.e. reports. Prior to taking this job, I had learned the maxim 'Reports are company specific.' I learned from these seven finance directors that reports (as in layout and content) are neither company-specific, nor site-specific, nor division-specific, but are unique to each of God's children under the sun, and this is most telling when it comes to finance directors.

143

During the year and a half that it took to implement the software in all of the sites, I spent an unholy amount of time huddled over sample cash flow analyses, aged debtor lists, and invoice reconciliation lists, while listening to the heads of *buchaltung, la comptabilite*, accounting, et al explain to me the merits of their, ultimately, person-specific way of doing their jobs. Young as I was at the time, I took these finance directors as seriously as they took themselves, and nearly drove  my programmer-analysts mad with 'system enhancement requests' pertaining to additional report lay-out options. In the final analysis we had seven aged debtors lists (brides) for seven finance directors (brothers), none of which lists distinguished itself in any viable fashion. Herr, monsieur, signor, senor, sir. At the end of this exercise, the European finance director weighed in with *his* opinion and I gave him the one piece of my mind that was left to me.

Scroll the years forward to the edge of the millenium and much has changed. IS no longer reports to Finance (hallelujah) and, in the world of SAP, IS is in a support role rather than direct-service role (much rejoicing), but one element of the nasty old past is still there: report lay-outs and content are still person-specific. Sort by client, sub-total by region by client type, include percentage of total and percentage of sub-total, and repeat all sub-totals by region with a grand total on the final, separate page.

My response in subsequent years was to include report generation capacity in any system I designed or implemented, offering users (royal or otherwise) the option of defining required data, the layout in which it would be presented, and a variety of data manipulation keys so that most desired reports could be generated by those who wanted specific information for specific needs.

This, too, failed to satisfy in any absolute way. What was requested, no, *insisted upon*, was a push-of-a-button solution, or better, a simple delivery of desired reports on a regular basis.

Excuse me. Please brush away that drift of my gray hair that has settled onto this page. And now, back to the fray...

You are advised to avoid lengthy discussions about reporting during an SAP implementation. 'Output' is the obsession of most users and is the least difficult element of SAP to satisfy. SAPScript is available, as well as hundreds of standard reports, Query functions, you name it. The occasional ABAP/4 program needs to be written, but for the most part, output should not be the subject. Again, the subject is workflow.

How you bring the subject back to workflow is up to a) your consulting talents, b) your understanding of the project at hand, and c) your audience. Be prepared to demonstrate SAP's formidable reporting capacity. In the course of system demonstrations, be prepared to song-and-dance this capacity to an exaggerated degree in the hopes of satisfying user concerns about anticipated *output*. Do not promise customized report layouts. Be a missionary, not a slave. If customized reports are the subject of a
meeting during BPR, you are so far off the critical path that a full fleet of Saint Bernards will not find you.

The paperless company is the dream of Brazilian forests. All the same, do what you can to convert your staff toward the use of screen query and the drill-down capacity of SAP. This is best accomplished if you have a solid understanding of the new business processes and are capable of demonstrating them in a prototypical fashion. Your ability to 'walk through' a process with people will do you all a great service. Saplings in the highlands will bless you, as will your implementation budget, and the state of your nervous system.

Another Change of Tune for Those Pesky Finance Directors

Invoicing has, since accounting time immemorial, been the domain of finance/accounting departments. Sales invoices have been generated by accounting. Purchase invoices have been gathered by accounting and married to delivery receipts before payment of such invoices has taken place. Sales invoices married to delivery notes lead to the collection process. All hail accounting. The scoreboard is all.

Better business practices (SAP says 'best,' but such distinctions are usually argued in North America) agree that invoicing of clients belongs to Sales & Distribution (SD) and purchase invoicing belongs to Materials Management (MM). With SAP, finance/accounting is the scorekeeper at last, and the players, i.e. the buyers and sellers, master the game of buying and selling.

You will have to be smooth, diplomatic, and firm while you WRENCH invoicing (sales and purchasing) from the scorekeepers and render it to those who know what to do with it.

Fewer Coaches and More Players

The flattening of vertical organizations into more horizontally-oriented organizations is the basic preoccupation of the business process reengineering that should accompany your project. The obvious outcome will be that there will be fewer middle managers in the immediate vicinity, and more players making up their own minds as to what has to be done and when.

The business assumption in North America since the 1950s has been that a business is like a football team, with everyone working a specific position, led by a quarterback, a head coach, a line coach, a receiver's coach, a defensive backfield coach, and (oh, those 1980s) a shrink. The football team concept was laid low by the Japanese wave of the 1980s in which these notions of managerial checks and balances were exposed as fat, slow, and somewhat pointless.

With SAP, you are entering into a phase in which even the notion of teaming is no longer the same as what you have known heretofore. Those line coaches and receiver coaches will disappear. Teams will become jazz ensembles or orchestras, forming and reforming according to need and opportunity, and then disbanding  once the need has been satisfied or the opportunity pounced-upon. Need will be business circumstance and opportunity will be the functional capacity and flexibility of SAP. In place of a brace of coaches will be a basic conductor, someone (or a much smaller group of someones) who will hold a baton to orchestrate the wave of activity that will characterize your working day.

Well beyond the implementation project, this factor will be your greatest collective challenge. How quickly will you and your tribe reform yourselves into a jazz ensemble? What level of resistance will you receive from the displaced management layers? How seriously will your upper management address this revolution? Finally, since every revolution leads to a counter-revolution, how will you deal with the backlash that this project will certainly inspire?

A few hints:

1. Be prepared to demonstrate the future; use the prototype as it develops, and organize walk-throughs of new business processes. In essence, prove the theory wherever possible.

2. Avoid demagoguery. You are not leading a revolt of the masses, merely helping your firm (or client) into the new millenium of business practices and supports.

3. Insist upon cost/benefit from angle to angle. Cost is easy to argue against; arguments again demonstrable benefit tend to melt like Arizona snow.

4. When arguing cultural changes, admit freely that the subject is culture. Company traditions are cultural as well and the battlefield will be leveled to matters at hand. Timidity disguised as caution will be ever-present and if you come down as heavy-handed, you will win many a battle while losing the war. Demonstrate, illustrate, and, more than anything else, predict the resistance you will encounter. Be prepare to lose a battle or two or three. Resistance is not always refusal. It is sometimes enlightenment, and, in its own way, teamwork..

All Martyrs Have One Thing in Common

They die ugly deaths. Saints or fools, they die.

The ideas of saints live on. The ideas of fools die with them. In the context of a company, all martyrs are fools. You do not have to push the envelope of your SAP/BPR cause with threats of resignation. If you do, your ideas will not survive your good-bye party.

Your CEO Knows Very Little About SAP. It's OK.

The top dog in your company has a lot to do that does not touch, or even approach, this year's bottom line. The CEO has bigger fish to fry than how you and your tribe do your business. Well, no, not bigger fish, just the fish that most CEOs think are bigger fish. Market share, mergers, joint ventures, media events, product diversification, board skirmishes, and the like tend to take up CEO time far more than business process reengineering.

Your CEO may be 'committed' to an SAP implementation, and may even back up this commitment with memos and declarations and the occasional brown-bag meeting. But the push of corporate navigation often tends to override the shove of internal renaissance.

If you can do so, educate your CEO. If not, seek to keep the CEO from mucking up the whole deal. This is not to say that CEOs are evil or ignorant or negligent. This is to say that CEOs tend to have other agendas, and SAP implementations are still viewed as structural adjustments rather than cultural revolutions. Woe unto them, but, hey, that is the way it usually goes. Mom and Dad are at the movies while you crazy kids are rearranging the house into a better place to live .

We do not mean to be capricious here. The job of a CEO, as defined in these times, has little to do with business process or business process reengineering. Your helpers at the top of the food chain are likely to be limited to the CFO, the COO, and the CIO, and various others of the same second concentric circle. So work the functionaries and the architects of the company, and the royalty, if you can do so.

Just a note, and a curious one at that. CIOs are not always a part of SAP implementations; indeed, they are often interested spectators, busily concerned with legacy systems while cheering on a parallel SAP project and hedging their bets both ways. If SAP fails, the legacy systems will remain and the CIO will be bruised but alive. If the SAP projects succeeds, the CIO gets interviewed by ComputerWorld and offers a few pithy phrases about the keys to success.

So, bring the CIO firmly into the SAP camp or prepare for longer hours and a higher mortality rate. If you fail to bring the CIO into the project, you may well succeed, and wildly so, but the success may be overturned, or ignored, or compromised beyond recognition.

If you *are* the CIO, great. You are in a prime position to assure project success. The key will be turning your attention ever more to SAP and ever less to the legacy systems. Those legacy systems may be the results of your own past labors and letting them go can be painful. The project team will be watching you and measuring your willingness to cut bait. Demonstrate your resolve and the path to SAP success will be straight.

The User is the User; You Are the Bringer of Light

Users are taught, guided, fooled, manipulated, and pummeled by change. They are not in command of the SAP implementation nor are they at the core of business process design decisions.

There is, in North America, an attitude that the 'user is right.' The user alone is not right. The user is a player on a team. Treat the 'user' as a human being with a job that was defined, refined, and supervised well before you showed up with your fancy-schmantzy ideas about ess ay pee and business process reengineering and its consequent 'empowerment.'

The people who will bang the keyboards will drive the system in ways that will defy your process charts. They will tend to rely on what they have done in the years that preceded *this* project. They will have seen programmer-analysts come and go; they will have read management memos that did or did not bear fruit; they will have filled out forms for no apparent reason; and they will have been gathered in conference rooms to listen to management initiatives about total quality management that were like grapes which never turned into wine. In short, you have a tough crowd to work and the changes inherent in an SAP project will only make it tougher.

SAP may be a career blow to people who suffer change badly. Or it may be a career kiss for those who roll with the punches tend to survive and prosper. Learning the Internet is a big deal to many people. Learning workflow is a far greater achievement.

Responsibility and contribution are at the core of what end users should provide. Do not tag these people with empty labels like

151

'empowerment'. Power is not what you are providing; you are providing opportunity and responsibility. Whether or not your management is capable of recognizing this will be a key to your mid and long-term success. If you give responsibility to those who have never had it, be prepared to cover for failures and be prepared to crown successes with recognition.

Your cultural task is your main task. Master the key phrases, the benefits-driven arguments, and the demonstration of the same, and your life will be silk-surrounded, and the usual thorns will turn to flowers. Or as close to a facsimile of flowers that business can provide.

A Roadkill A to Z

*Identifying Failure in SAP Implementations
and Recognizing the Success*

Failure Is a Moment, Success is a Season

A lie gets halfway around the world before the truth puts its boots on.

Winston Churchill

Your ultimate success or failure will, in all reality, be in the eye of the beholder. Few projects of the grandeur of an enterprise-wide applications suite implementation will be perceived wholly as one or the other. In the Black Hills of South Dakota is the largest gold mine in North America. This mine has existed for 120 years. Where once was a green and majestic mountain, there is now only a dusty plain. Billions of 1997 dollars have been blasted and sifted and in our business world this mine has been mighty darn successful; yet that majestic mountain is no more. It is a void; it is gone forever.

We have read of countless SAP failures in the press, but when we re-read the articles, we find that the implementation game is still afoot. Clients have become testy and both budgets and nerves are stretched thin; yet the projects are still continuing and implementation teams are being formed or reformed. Failure to implement SAP in six months or a year is too often viewed as total failure, and this attitude, based as it is on historical and classical *single application* implementations, is both unfair and shortsighted; unfair to the companies and the people involved, and shortsighted when it comes to SAP.

I have mined my memory as fully as that blasted mountain to remember which witless 1960's football coach came up with the phrase: show me a good loser and I will show you a loser. The notion of winning or losing, success or failure, is a lobotomized simplification of what we do in the intricate and human fields of business. Consider, in an SAP implementation, the various blends of failure or success that might occur:

- SAP was licensed but not implemented; i.e. was not used at all;

- SAP was implemented, but the project was over budget and/or late;

- SAP was partially implemented, meaning some legacy systems are still in use;

- SAP was implemented but the results are not what were expected by those who had the wrong expectations;

- SAP is being implemented, but no one knows why or how.

Of these categories, the only ultimate failure is the first, but even so, a failure to use SAP whatsoever may be instructive and proper, and, in its own light, a success. In the new, revised and expanded version of our first book, *In the Path of the Whirlwind, An Apprentice Guide to the World of SAP*, we offer a thorough question-and-answer inventory of 'Are You Ready for SAP?' Many companies will prove in this simple inventory that they are not ready. Companies which are visibly and stubbornly vertical will fail at SAP implementations as surely as the rain will fall in Scotland in March. Companies with poor management vision will put their SAP teams behind the eight ball with the stroke of a budget-revision.

And yet, success comes in odd forms once we view success as a significant and tangible progress towards workflow.

We have long observed one huge firm that has groaned and moaned through an SAP implementation, a firm that has spent millions on consultants, travel, meetings, you name it, and still has not seen much in the way of progress. The failure to implement SAP is a fog in the hallways, but a certain scent of success has begun to waft into that fog. This company is a veritable collection of vertical empires, and we suspect that the SAP implementation project is the club that the CEO has chosen to flatten those vertical empires in order to hammer his company into fighting trim.

As a result of the SAP project, the company is now engaged in heated debate as to how it will proceed into the next quarter century, and not how it will continue business as usual. Whether or not this company succeeds in implementing SAP according to the massive wall charts that can be seen in a variety of its offices is not entirely the point. It is now a question of workflow vs. the way we were. The advancement of pawns has long since given way to the toppling of knights and bishops. We suspect that within a year or so, the company culture will become stained with the ink of progress, and an SAP implementation, or some version thereof, will occur. In the interim, failure is the verdict. Success is only the rumor, the truth that has not yet put on its boots.

The Consulting Alliance

The Brains, The Heart, The Courage

Toto, I Have a Feeling We're Not in Kansas Anymore

When L. Frank Baum lived in Aberdeen, South Dakota, he wrote and distributed his first version of *The Wizard of Oz*, and his friends and neighbors were offended by his descriptions of South Dakota as a flat and desolate place. To boost readership and promote neighborly relations, he rewrote the book with a Kansas locale. In the wake of the success of the book and film, it has been wrongly assumed that Kansas was the starting point for that yellow brick road journey to Oz. It was South Dakota. In our recent technological times, South Dakota has given you the computer company, Gateway 2000®, with its rural motif, cows, and black and white boxes. This place of Oz is a technological Gateway—a most certain and reliable starting point on your trek toward SAP success.

Although the immovable stone faces of Mt. Rushmore reside in South Dakota, **THE CONSULTING ALLIANCE** is a global organization with offices or projects on four (4) continents—Europe, North America, South America, and Asia-Pacific. Our consultants and instructors hail from places such as Hamburg, Atlanta, Philadelphia, Rapid City,

Cleveland, Fargo, Munich, Winnipeg, Hong Kong, Shanghai and countless other points on the globe. We have successfully implemented SAP countless times, either as lead consultants or as partners in multi-partner projects. We rely upon experience, method, tools, and grace. We are not a family, we are a tribe. And we have a habit of succeeding.

In sum, THE CONSULTING ALLIANCE is a single-source company offering an *Integrated Approach™* to companies seeking to implement and use SAP products. The *Integrated Approach™* **underscores the necessity of an SAP education—the transfer of SAP knowledge—** from our staff to the client staff from the commencement of the project through the implementation.

Its consulting group is known as **THE OR PARTNER GROUP,** which means "Organization and Reengineering Partner". Our consultant profile is an average age of 35, with 4 ½ years of SAP experience preceded by eleven years of industry experience. We offer SAP implementation and strategic consulting services. That is all we do. We follow SAP's guidelines for implementation according to the ASAP project approach that has been approved by SAP. THE OR PARTNER GROUP has offices in Germany, the U.S., and China.

We believe that a more complete SAP education is the essential missing link to successful SAP implementations. Through the use of **THE DOLPHIN GROUP'S** educational services, we complement SAP applications courses and strive for client self-sufficiency and, ultimately, client independence. THE DOLPHIN GROUP, with its Education Center in Wilmington, Delaware, offers seminars and courses for all levels of your company: executive-level, project managers, coordinators, and direct users. Our instructors are consultants who have distinguished themselves in the field and all have legitimate SAP implementation experience and background.

- *In the Path of the Whirlwind*^{TM}: An Executive Course in SAP.

- *Capturing the Whirlwind*^{TM}: Your Field Guide for a Successful SAP Implementation.

- Dolphin 2000™: 10 days of hands-on training from FI-CO to SD-MM and an integration test during which students build and test a functioning model company with SAP.

- Dolphin 4000™: a team-oriented configuration and integration workshop; 10 days of learning by doing: students learn to configure an R/3 system (FI, CO, SD, MM, PP, and HR) by building a functional model based upon a case study. A true microcosm of an SAP implementation.

- Dolphin 5000™: a team-oriented configuration and integration workshop; 5 days of learning by doing: students learn to configure an R/3 system (FI, CO, SD, MM,) by building a functional model based upon a case study. A true microcosm of an SAP implementation.

- Courses customized for the clients using our standard course offerings as a foundation.

THE CONSULTING ALLIANCE also publishes and distributes *In the Path of the Whirlwind, An Apprentice Guide to the World of SAP which is now in its fourth printing.* Amoco, Georgia Pacific, Dupont, IBM, Deloitte/ICS, Texaco, Andersen Consulting, SAP and other companies have ordered this book more than once. What are they reading?

In plain, often blunt, language, this book looks beyond the hearsay and misinformation, and provides answers to these and other questions:

- Why is SAP so hot?

- Is SAP a fad or a phenomenon?

- Is SAP only for Fortune 500 companies?

- Why is SAP so difficult to implement?

- How much re-engineering of business processes is needed to implement SAP?

- What are the hidden costs of an SAP project?

- What is the optimal use of consultants in an SAP project?

- Why are experienced SAP consultants so hard to find?

- Is SAP your downsizing partner?

The tag line of THE DOLPHIN GROUP is *Helping Humans Adapt to SAP.* Humans have much to adapt to during an SAP implementation—much to learn, much to endure. In honor of the Dolphins, we will publish in the early summer of 1997 a new book called *People in the Whirlwind: The Human Side of An SAP Implementation.* Coming soon to a theater near you.

Reaping the Whirlwind: Obtaining the Most Benefits from Your SAP Implementation may be forthcoming this year or in 1998.

If you liked this book, call us. If you take issue with this book, call us. If you would like more of the same, call us. If you want more books, call us. We have telephone numbers, we have fax machines galore, and we are at the ready.

And, no, Toto, we are not in Kansas anymore. South Dakota. We are on the map. If you wish to find the Oz of SAP, this is a good place to begin your journey. We would like to go with you on your journey.

Contact us: Wolfgang Beitz, Managing Partner
                     Chris J. Carlsen, Managing Partner
                     The CONSULTING ALLIANCE, L.L.C.
                     101 South Main Avenue, 6th Floor
                     Sioux Falls, SD, USA 57104-6423
                     Phone (605) 339-3074 or (888) 466-8244
                     Internet: www.tcall.com

Field Guide Help Pages and Notes

SAP Application ID's:

CO	Controlling	
FI	Financial Accounting	
	EC	Enterprise Controlling
	IM	Capital Investment Management
	AM	Assets Management
	TR	Treasury
HR	Human Resources	
	PA	Personnel Application
	PD	Personnel Planning & Development
LO	Logistics	
	MM	Materials Management
	PM	Plant Maintenance
	PP	Production Planning
	PS	Project System
	QM	Quality Management
	SD	Sales & Distribution

Basis   The middleware which smoothes operations across the variety of possible operating systems

ABAP/4 The programming language used

Terms and Acronyms

ABAP	Advanced Business Application Programming Language
AM	Fixed Assets Management application in SAP
ASAP	No, we say *an* SAP
ASAP	An SAP method for rapid implementation, sort of
Business Process	a group or series of activities by which inputs are turned to outputs that benefit the customer
C/S	Client/server
CO	Controlling application in SAP
Customize	making changes to the system that will fit your process designs
FI	Financial application in SAP
Gap analysis	the analysis of what you want to do that you think won't be provided by SAP
GUI	Graphical User Interface
HR	Human Resources application in SAP
ICOE	Industry Centers of Expertise
Interfaces	Program-driven connections between disparate data bases
IS	Information systems
IS	Industry Solutions application in SAP
Middleware (Basis)	The / between client and server, as in Client/Server
MM	Materials management application
OC	Office & Communications application in SAP
OR	Organization & Reengineering Partner OR Partner
PM	Production Maintenance application in SAP
Portability	the capacity of software to be run on various operating systems
PP	Production Planning application in SAP
PS	Project System application in SAP
QA	Quality Assurance in SAP
QM	Quality Management application in SAP
SAP	Ess Ay Pee
SD	Sales and distribution application in SAP
Software suite	multiple software applications derived from common design

Internet Notes

Someone once compared the evolution of the Internet to that of the Far West, adding that each year is like ten years of Western history. If so, we are now at about 1890 and have another ten years of wildness, lawlessness, mountains, deserts, bandits, and rattlesnakes to endure.

SAP itself has a site on the Internet (SAP.Com) that could be likened to San Francisco in the 1890's. A bit gaudy, a touch proud, but rich in helpful information about the company, the product, the consulting partners, and the clients who have implemented. A recent addition is a library of success stories, offering full color short-sheets on the companies that have implemented SAP and what they got out of it. Though these sheets reek of market-speak, it is useful to see what has been accomplished throughout the world.

There are scores of other sites relative to SAP, sites which offer technical background, detail about the Business Engineering Workbench, help note sites for implementers, ABAP notes sites, and more. We will not list them here because too many will disappear or re-locate or merge by the time you read this book. What is important to know is that there are hundreds of them and you need only to use a basic search engine like Lycos or Yahoo to find them.

While you are implementing, it is recommended that you check out the SAP.com site on a regular basis. As already mentioned, new announcements are daily and new releases almost monthly. Do not over-react to the announcements; many are pre-mature and many others are responses to magazines articles couched as fact. Still, with those thousand munchkins crunching new SAP code on a daily basis, you had best remain informed as to where they are headed.

A Final Note: Do You Have A Major Problem?—19YY

In 1976 while working for the City of St. Paul, Minnesota, I was instructed to design and program a system that would capture and track all bonded debt for the city. Having settled the functional specifications with a withered but kind city accountant, I hunkered down to the COBOL programs required to fulfill those requirements. My first test program was for a twenty-five year bond, and the re-payment and interest tables that I made with COBOL programs worked just fine until the next to the last year. That year was 2000.

Up until that time, my use of a two-digit year figure was sufficient for the payment calculations, but suddenly 00 minus 99 did not yield the expected answer of '1'. I ran smack into a problem that is now, twenty-some years later, preoccupying scores of companies—the once important, and now totally insignificant, need to save two the lousy digits '19' in any date field included in a record. Why enter 1967 when 67 works just as well? Had I started my bond project in 1974 rather than 1976, I probably would not have learned this lesson—19YY.

I was fortunate in 1976 to find a solution which I could use in future projects. You may be fortunate, too. The pain of 19YY provides another cost consideration in the realm of SAP. SAP thought ahead and deals with this situation for centuries to come. If you are still considering an SAP implementation, you might take into account the potential savings of not having to modify your existing programs. A recent U.S. government announcement reveals that over two billions dollars have been budgeted for the correction of this problem. We do not know the size of your company's 19YY budget. But considering the whatever the size of the budget, maybe you should have implemented SAP. Just maybe.